INSIGHT COMPACT GUIDES

MUNICH

GREAT LITTLE GUIDES

Compact Guide: Munich is the ideal quick-reference guide to the Bavarian capital. It tells you everything you need to know about Munich's attractions, from the bustle of Marienplatz to the tranquillity of the English Garden, from the pleasures of the city's beer gardens to the treasures of its museums.

This is one of almost 100 titles in *Insight Guides'* series of pocket-sized, easy-to-use guidebooks intended for the independent-minded traveller. *Compact Guides* are in essence travel encyclopedias in miniature, designed to be comprehensive yet portable, as well as up-to-date and authoritative.

SO-CBV-260

Star Attractions

An instant reference
to some of Munich's
most popular tourist
attractions to help
you on your way.

Marienplatz p16

Asamkirche p20

Hofbräuhaus p24

Deutsches Museum p25

English Garden p40

Municipal Gallery p46

Oktoberfest p58

The Zoo p62

Olympic Park p60

MUNICH

Introduction

Places

Culture

Leisure

Practical Information

Munich – world city with a heart

The art of living and letting live is one of the many secrets of Munich, which for centuries has attracted people from all parts of Germany, and from all of Europe, and given them a warm welcome. This secret is well expressed by Munich's oft-repeated nickname: 'Weltstadt mit Herz' (world city with a heart).

But what is Munich? Hofbräuhaus, Oktoberfest, Schwabing, Bavarian hospitality? All this is part of it. But Munich is really so much more. Munich is one of Germany's cultural capitals, unrivalled by any except Berlin in the areas of classical music and opera, fine art museums, theatre, and film. It is also an extremely beautiful city, whose churches, facades and broad tree-lined avenues bear magnificent testimony to a long, eventful, and mostly prosperous past.

The Münchner Kindl – Munich's mascot

It's no coincidence that half of the German population, given a choice, would rather be living in Munich. The city radiates an atmosphere which not only attracts strangers but also holds them. Native born citizens of Munich have become a rarity, but the number of people who regard themselves as Munich citizens in spirit is much greater. After World War II the Bavarian capital had the highest growth rate of all the big cities in the German Federal Republic.

5

Munich's power of attraction lies in the fact that its opposites can unite and its extremes can become reconciled. The most divergent philosophies of life exist peacefully side by side. Baroque zest for living is paired with traditional piety. The exuberance of *Fasching (carnival)* harmonises with the festive solemnity of a Corpus Christi procession. The 'village of a million inhabitants' is as well-known for its high-tech industry as it is for its shady beer gardens. Avant-garde art competes with the world-class works of art on exhibit in the city's galleries. In addition to concerts by world-famous composers, there is lively culture in the city's various districts.

Not the least of the reasons for Munich's popularity, however, is its wonderful surroundings. The city is less than an hour from the Alps, surrounded by lakes, near to Austria, Italy and Switzerland. Hikers, hang-gliders and watersports enthusiasts are in their element in the summer months, whilst in the winter the slopes become the preserve of skiers and tobogganists.

Position and size

Munich is the capital of Bavaria and of the administrative district of Upper Bavaria. It lies on a plain belonging to the Bavarian Alpine Foreland (foothills). Munich is about 530m (1,700ft) above sea level; from this point the

The Isar flows through the heart of the city

country falls gradually towards the north until the Danube is reached. The Isar, which originates in the Alps about 90km (55 miles) away, flows through the town from south to north. The core of the old city is on the left, western bank of the river. Visitors are often surprised to see such a clean river flowing right through the heart of a city.

The present population of the city, which covers about 310sq km (120sq miles), is some 1,200,000. The Bavarian metropolis is the third-largest city in Germany, trailing only Berlin and Hamburg.

Climate

Because of Munich's proximity to the northern edge of the Alps, precipitation is rather high. Rain storms often come violently and unexpectedly. The range of temperatures between day and night and between summer and winter can be extreme. Even during a single season there are often drastic changes in temperature. A period of bad weather in summer can push the mercury below the level of a spring day which has been warmed by the *Föhn*.

The *Föhn* is a famous and feared climatic feature, which manages to change not only the weather and the temperature completely within a few hours, but also, very often, the mood of the people. Many in Munich tend to blame this warm southerly wind whenever they don't feel well or find themselves in an irritable mood. Whenever there is an unusually frequent spate of traffic accidents, this also tends to get blamed on the *Föhn*. The wind originates when there is a ridge of high pressure on the south side of the Alps (Italy) and a low pressure area on the north side. The air from the south descends as a warm wind through the Alpine Foreland as far as the Danube. In times of *Föhn* the Alps viewed from Munich almost seem close enough to touch. There is a saying that you can sometimes see the whites of the eyes of the sheep roaming the mountains.

Traditional attire

Population

The character of the so-called *Altmünchner* (native of Munich), is often depicted in clichés – mostly incorrect and exaggerated – as being one of brashness, craftiness, and bad temper. The big city Bavarian mentality is stamped by a strongly conservative ideology, the main reason for which is a deep-rooted individualism; the original Bavarian intensely dislikes having his individuality threatened by modernistic trends.

The fact that the German population of Munich is divided almost exactly in half between *Zuag' roasten* (immigrants) and native inhabitants can be heard clearly in speech. Everywhere in the city what is called Munich High German can be heard. The old Bavarian dialect is linguistically similar to the language spoken in Austria.

Religion

Munich is a predominantly Roman Catholic city and has been the seat of the Archbishop of Munich and Freising since 1821. Religious observances play an important role for many of the people and most of the customs which still colour the seasons of the year have their roots in traditional Catholic piety.

Government and administration

Munich is the capital of Bavaria and of the administrative district of Upper Bavaria. For this reason it is the seat of many institutions: the Landtag (Parliament), the Senate, the Bavarian State Government, the Highest Bavarian Law Court, the Bavarian Constitutional Court, the Bavarian Administrative Court, the District Council, the Government of Upper Bavaria. Also included are several federal offices such as the Federal Finance Audit Office, the German Patent Office (Munich is even the seat of the European Patent Office). Furthermore, the city is also the seat of various religious dignitaries.

The Munich flag

Economy

Munich is the second largest industrial city in the German Federal Republic. Names like Siemens, BMW, Krauss-Maffei, MAN, Rathgeber, MBB, MTU, Linhof and Rodenstock are closely connected with Munich. Of considerable economic importance also are the Munich breweries: there are six major ones. The above-mentioned companies are supplemented by important chemical, printing, and clothing industries.

The significance of Munich as a financial centre is proved by its more than 100 banks. There are also 35 insurance companies situated here. Because of numerous special trade exhibitions, Munich is regarded as an international centre in this field, too. With 300 firms producing books, Munich has more publishing houses than any other city in the Federal Republic of Germany.

Knowledge and research

The Ludwig-Maximilians-Universität and the Technical University have together more than 80,000 students. In addition to these two universities there are the Military Academy, the School of Philosophy, the State Academy of Music, the Academy for Television and Film, the Academy of Visual Art, the Bavarian Academy of Science and the Bavarian Academy of the Fine Arts, as well as numerous technical colleges.

The largest library in the German Federal Republic is the Bavarian State Library, with more than seven million books, followed by the University Library (over two million books).

Historical Highlights

About 1200BC The Illyrians, who had come from southeastern Europe, settled on the northern edge of the Alps. From the 5th century BC Celts penetrated the Alpine Foreland from the west.

15BC The Romans under Tiberius and Drusus thrust forward to the Danube.

C AD500 After a short period of Ostrogothic rule, the country begins to be settled by the Baiuvarii from Bohemia.

746 The monastery at Tegernsee is founded, and a small branch of it on the Isar is given the name *Munichen* (the home of the monks). The name first appears in a document in 777.

907–37 Arnulf (from the House of Luitpolding) succeeds in renewing the local duchy.

947 Bavaria falls to the Saxons under Otto I, who awards the duchy to his brother Heinrich.

1070 The Welfs become dukes of Bavaria.

1158 Henry the Lion, the last and most famous of the Welf dukes, founds Munich. In 1156 he destroys the bridge over the Isar at Oberföhring (which belongs to the bishop of Freising and brings in a vast toll) and builds a new one a few kilometres up river near Munichen, where he collects the toll himself. The brisk salt trade from Reichenhall and Hallein ensures a profitable income. Henry the Lion moves with mint and market to Munichen. After Emperor Frederick I (Barbarossa) sanctions the results of Henry's manoeuvring at the Reichstag (imperial diet) in Augsburg, Munich is born. The official date: 14 June 1158.

1180 Henry the Lion falls under the imperial ban for denying Frederick Barbarossa military loyalty. The Hohenstaufen emperor rewards his loyal vassal Otto von Wittelsbach with the duchy of Bavaria.

1255 Duke Ludwig II (the Stern) receives the Palatinate and Upper Bavaria as his part in the first partition of Bavaria. He chooses Munich as capital and royal seat of his section of the duchy.

1302 Duke Ludwig the Bavarian begins his rule (from 1328 emperor, German king from 1314).

He builds a second ring of walls around Munich; the construction takes 15 years.

1327 Munich falls victim to a devastating fire.

1392 The third partition of Bavaria occurs. The country is divided into the duchies of Ingolstadt, Landshut, and Munich.

1397–8 An uprising of the artisans and small tradesmen, which is repeated several times in the succeeding period, helps the burghers to gain a greater share in local government.

1429 Part of the town is burnt down.

1506 Duke Albrecht IV (the Wise) issues a decree enforcing primogeniture, thereby initiating the end of Bavaria's partition. Munich becomes the capital of the whole of Bavaria.

1508–50 The reign of Duke Wilhelm IV, who strongly opposes the Reformation in Bavaria. Shortly before his death in 1549 he summons the Jesuits to Bavaria, which becomes an important stronghold of the Counter-Reformation.

1550–79 Duke Albrecht V succeeds in making Catholicism the exclusive religion of Bavaria through the 1555 Peace of Augsburg. The duke encourages art and learning.

1598 Duke Maximilian I becomes ruler of Bavaria. In 1609 he founds the Catholic League, which he leads during the Thirty Years War. In 1623 Maximilian is rewarded with the electorate of the Palatinate.

1632 The armies of King Gustav Adolph of Sweden occupy Munich.

1634 The imperial Spanish troops enter Munich. Plague and the confusions of the Thirty Years War reduce the population from 22,000 to 9,000.

1704–14 In the War of Spanish Succession Elector Maximilian II Emanuel, who takes sides with France, loses the whole of Bavaria to the Austrians. In 1705 peasants rise against the Austrian occupying force, only to be massacred by imperial troops in 'the murderous Christmas of Sendling'.

Maximilian II Emanuel receives Bavaria back without loss of territory at the peace conference of 1714.

1742 The Wittelsbach Karl Albrecht is elected emperor in Frankfurt and becomes Charles VII.

1745–77 His son Maximilian III rules in Bavaria. He makes peace with Austria, renouncing his hereditary titles and assures three decades of peace, devoting himself to the demands of learning and the construction of his state.

1777–99 Karl Theodor rules a Bavaria that includes the Upper Palatinate but not the Innviertel.

1799–1825 Bavaria is ruled by Maximilian IV Joseph from the Palatinate-Zweibrücken line. As compensation for areas left of the Rhine (incorporated with Bavaria by Karl Theodor) ceded to Napoleon, Bavaria receives the secularised bishoprics Würzburg, Bamberg, Augsburg, Freising, and Passau at a peace treaty with France in 1803.

1805 Napoleon makes Munich his headquarters. After the battle of Austerlitz he transfers the margravate Ansbach-Bayreuth to Bavaria, as well as the Austrian territories of Vorarlberg, Tyrol, Salzburg, Innviertel and Hausruckviertel.

1806 Maximilian IV Joseph receives the title of king as a favour from Napoleon and from then on calls himself Maximilian I Joseph.

1815 Bavaria joins the German Confederation.

1818 Maximilian I Joseph proclaims the Bavarian constitution.

1825 King Ludwig I comes to the throne. Under his rule Munich becomes a brilliant and thriving centre of art and learning.

1840 The railway line from Munich to Augsburg is inaugurated.

1848 The revolution of 1848, sparked off in Bavaria partly by the king's love affair with a young Irish dancer from Limerick named Lola Montez, leads to Ludwig I's abdication.

1848–64 His son Maximilian II reigns. He fosters art and learning and introduces important innovations in the sphere of social reform

1864–86 The reign of King Ludwig II, the fairy-tale king, builder of fantastic castles. Under him Bavaria takes the side of Austria in the Seven Weeks War against Prussia (1866) and that of Prussia in the Franco–German War (1870–1). Ludwig is found drowned in Lake Starnberg.

1886–1912 Prince Regent Luitpold rules in place of Ludwig's mentally disturbed brother.

1918–19 The last reigning Wittelsbach, King Ludwig III, is deposed in the November revolution. The socialist Kurt Eisner becomes Bavaria's first prime minister, proclaiming a 'Free People's Republic'. The ensuing months see the assassination of Eisner, the establishment of a soviet republic, or *Räterepublik*, and its violent overthrow at the hands of the conservative White Guard. The storm dies down when the Bamberg Constitution officially terms Bavaria a 'Free State and Member of the German Empire'.

1923 An attempted National Socialist (Nazi) putsch put down in front of the Feldherrnhalle. Hitler is imprisoned at Landsberg.

1933 The National Socialists remove the last legally elected city council on 9 March. Munich becomes the 'Capital of the Movement'.

1938 The Munich Agreement, signed here by Hitler, Mussolini, Chamberlain, and Daladier, seals the destruction of Czechoslovakia.

1943 A gallant group of university students and professors, known as the White Rose, revolt against the tyranny of the Third Reich.

1945 Having sustained heavy damage by allied bombers, Munich is taken by American troops without resistance.

1946 The constitution of the Bavarian Free State is approved by the people.

1957 Munich's population reaches one million.

1972 The XX Olympic Games held in the city.

1992 The new Munich airport is opened.

1994 The 500th anniversary of the consecration of Munich's cathedral.

The fountain on Karlsplatz

Preceding pages:
view from St Peter's Church

Route 1

The city centre: Karlsplatz – Burgersaal – Old Academy – St Michael's Church – Hunting and Fishing Museum – Frauenkirche – Marienplatz

The route described below covers Munich's main artery, the main shopping and business centre. About two hours are needed for viewing this area in detail.

It begins in **Karlsplatz ❶**. The locals call this square 'Stachus', which is probably an abbreviation of the Christian name of Eustachius Föderl, who, from 1726 onwards, had a shooting inn here, just outside the city walls, which were then still standing. Karlsplatz was laid out in 1791, when Elector Karl Theodor (1777–99) ordered the city's fortifications to be torn down at various points and the moat filled in. Today there is a four-storey subterranean complex with modern shops in the upper storey. Karlsplatz is an important transport junction. It is only five minutes by foot from the main railway station and some 10 minutes from Marienplatz.

The Palace of Justice

To the north of the square is the Justizpalast (Palace of Justice or law courts), built in 1891–7 by Friedrich von Thiersch in a late-Renaissance and baroque style. On the east side the square is closed off by a semi-circle of buildings. In the middle – behind a modern fountain – is the **Karlstor**. This structure was the former west gate inside the second city fortification built under Ludwig the Bavarian (1314–47) and was called Neuhauser Tor. The towers standing today were rebuilt by Rumford when Elector Karl Theodor had the square laid out. Beyond, the pedestrian precinct, opened in 1972, extends along Neuhauser Strasse and Kaufinger Strasse.

Behind the gate on the left is the **Bürgersaal** ❷. Not consecrated as a church until 1778, the building was initially designed as a meeting place for the Men's Marian Congregation of Germany (a Jesuit organisation), a place for religious services and for the performance of sacred music. It was built in 1709–10 by Georg Ettenhofer according to the plans of Giovanni Antonio Viscardi.

The Bürgersaal

The main hall, the decoration of which was entrusted to Johann Georg Bader (stuccowork) and Johann Anton Gumpp (frescoes) in the 18th century, has been restored like the old Bürgersaal; between 1971 and 1980, stucco and wall and ceiling frescoes were created anew. On the side walls are 14 murals in oil by Franz Joachim Beich (1719), which depict the most famous Bavarian pilgrimages. Of Andreas Faistenberger's important high altar (1710) the war spared only the superb ★ *Annunciation* relief. One of Ignaz Günther's masterpieces is the ★ *Guardian Angel* sculpture (1763) under the gallery. The same artist created designs for the silver busts on the altar, which were made by Joseph Heinrich Kanzler in 1776.

13

On the ground floor, kept in almost total darkness, is the grave (1948) of the Munich Jesuit priest Rupert Mayer, who was deported to a concentration camp for his resistance to the Nazis and who died in 1945 from injuries sustained while in detention. He was beatified by the Pope in 1987.

Further along on the left, at Neuhauser Strasse 51, is the **Old Academy** ❸ (Alte Akademie). The noble and restrained facade of this former Jesuit college was built by Friedrich Sustris from 1585–97. Duke Wilhelm V sup-

Old Academy plaque

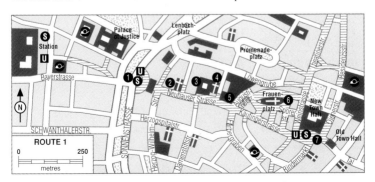

The Richard Strauss Fountain

The Church of St Michael

The barrel vaulted ceiling

ported the Jesuits, whom he had called to Munich in 1559, because he regarded them as the most potent weapon of the Counter-Reformation. After the dissolution of the Jesuit Order (in 1773 by Pope Clement XIV), the college was used, in turn, as the seat of the Academy of Sciences, the University (1826–40), the State Library (until 1843), the Academy of Fine Arts (until 1885) and the Bavarian Office of Statistics. The **Richard Strauss Fountain**, with its figure group from the opera *Salome* at the little square here, was designed by Hans Wimmer in remembrance of Munich's best-known musician, the composer of world-famous operas.

Duke Wilhelm V was also the founder of the nearby ★★ **Church of St Michael ❹**. Designed as a monument to the Counter-Reformation, St Michael's church was begun in 1583. After the tower collapsed in 1590, also causing damage to the choir section, the duke entrusted the Dutchman Friedrich Sustris with the completion of the church. Sustris, along with Wendel Dietrich, had already worked on the original construction under the direction of Wolfgang Müller. In 1597 the official consecration of the church took place. In World War II the church was seriously damaged. Rebuilding began in 1946.

The impressive facade was restored in 1972. Between the two portals there is a large niche with the bronze sculpture of ★ *St Michael vanquishing Satan*. The figure was modelled by Hubert Gerhard, the casting was made by Martin Frey (1592). In the other, smaller niches of the upper storeys and the gable stand the founder Wilhelm V (first storey, third from the right with the model church) and his Wittelsbach ancestors. The highest niche is reserved for Christ the Saviour.

At the time it was built, the ★ **interior** was regarded as an architectural sensation. Up to this point people were only familiar with the high-pillared Gothic naves, but now a gigantic Renaissance hall, 20m (66ft) wide, with a barrel vaulted ceiling, opened up before the eyes of the believers, creating a spatial effect which introduced the baroque concept of church design to Germany. At the time only St Peter's Cathedral in Rome had larger dimensions.

The stucco decorations of the partitioned barrel vault (Hubert Gerhard), which was destroyed in the war, were restored in 1981. The high altar was erected by Wendel Dietrich between 1586 and 1589. The altarpiece was created by Christoph Schwarz (1587). The four bronze reliefs are by Hubert Gerhard (about 1595). In the left transept is the ★ **tomb of Eugène de Beauharnais**, the stepson of Napoleon I and son-in-law of Maximilian I Joseph, which was executed by Bertel Thorvaldsen in 1830. In the right transept is the sculpture of *Mary Magdalen at the feet of Christ Crucified* by Giovanni da

Bologna. *The Martyrdom of St Ursula* and the *Annunciation* in the side chapel next to the transept were the work of Peter Candid. Duke Wilhelm V, Elector Maximilian I and King Ludwig II are buried in the vault under the choir.

On the corner of Neuhauser Strasse and Augustinerstrasse, you come to an impressive building, which is essentially a remnant of the Gothic era: the former **Augustinian Church ❺** . Between 1291 and 1294 the Augustinian friars built a church and monastery at this place, then still outside the city walls constructed by Henry the Lion. The church was greatly altered in the 14th, 15th, and 17th century. After the monastery was dissolved in 1803 the church was secularised, the hall being used as a customs house. Where the former monastery used to be are the present-day police headquarters. In 1911 construction of shops on the ground floor of the basilica began. Since 1966 the former church has served as the **Deutsches Jagd- und Fischereimuseum** (German Hunting and Fishing Museum) with collections of hunting weapons, trophies, paintings and drawings, splendid hunting sledges and a fishing section. Among the curiosities are the collection of documents concerning the story of the poacher Bayerischer Hiasl and the legendary Wolpertinger (a phantasmic animal consisting of parts of several other beasts, eg a cat, a fox, etc).

A Wolpertinger

Opposite the church, on the corner of the building where the clothing store Hirmer is located, is a little stone figure with the model of a tower. The model is a representation of the Schöner Turm (beautiful tower), which stood here until 1807 as part of the western boundary of Henry the Lion's Munich.

The curve of the Augustinerstrasse follows the line of the oldest city wall. Going along this street one soon reaches Frauenplatz, passes the granite-block fountain built by Bernhard Winkler in 1972 and is confronted by the west facade of the **★★ Frauenkirche ❻** . Its official name is Dom und Stadtpfarrkirche zu Unserer Lieben Frau (Cathedral and Parish Church of Our Lady). In 1468 the foundation of the cathedral was laid, after the Romanesque Marienkirche was torn down. The earlier church had replaced the old chapel of the Virgin, of uncertain date, which had been built before the founding of Munich. Jörg von Halspach, called Ganghofer, was entrusted with the construction of the cathedral. The vault was finished in 1477, the twin towers in 1488. The cupolas of the towers (100m/328ft and 99m/325ft high), which have become Munich's symbol, were not added until 1525. After the formation of the archbishopric of Munich and Freising (1821), the Frauenkirche became the cathedral of Munich. The cathedral was substantially renovated for the 500th

The Frauenkirche towers

anniversary of its consecration, which was celebrated in April 1994.

The general design of the main portal, as well as that of the other four doors, was by Ignaz Günther (1772); the sculptures of Christ and Madonna with Child on the side pedestals are from the Romanesque basilica. The pedestal figures of Christ and Mary at the St Benno Portal date from the 15th century. The figure of St Sebastian is by Andreas Faistenberger. The figures of Christ and Mary at the Bride's Portal date from 1430.

The interior of the church, which is among the largest hall churches in southern Germany, consists of three naves of equal height. Several of the Gothic stained-glass windows deserve to be mentioned: the Annunciation (1392), the Scharfzandt Window (made by Peter Hemmel von Andlau in 1493) and the Three Magi Window, which depicts the life of Jesus of Nazareth (1430). These windows are located in the choir gallery.

At the west end of the southern side aisle is the **★ tomb of Emperor Ludwig the Bavarian**. Maximilian I entrusted Hans Krumper with the project of the *Castrum doloris* in black marble. Krumper also created the bronze figures of Albrecht V and Wilhelm IV, while Hubert Gerhard designed the four guard figures.

Behind the choir some steps lead down to the **Princes' Vault**, the resting place of the Wittelsbach rulers, from the sons of Ludwig the Bavarian to Albrecht V. The last Bavarian king, Ludwig III, is also buried here. A second vault is reserved exclusively for the archbishops of Munich and Freising.

View from the top

On a clear day, visitors should consider taking the lift up the 98-m (322-ft) South Tower of the Frauenkirche, which offers a magnificent view of the city and its surroundings (Monday to Saturday 10am–5pm, closed on Sunday and public holidays; admission charge).

Marienplatz

Sporerstrasse leads through to Weinstrasse and to **★ ★ ★ Marienplatz ❼**. This square has been the urban centre of Munich since the foundation of the city in 1158. It has been called Marienplatz since 1854; before that the name was Schrannenmarkt or Schrannenplatz, the place where farmers and tradesmen sold their goods.

The entire north side of Marienplatz is taken up by the impressive **New Town Hall** (Neues Rathaus), which was constructed between 1867 and 1908 according to plans by Georg Hauberrisser. The main facade of the building, which is built around six courtyards in lavish neo-Gothic style, is adorned with figures representing Bavarian kings, electors, Munich 'originals', and characters from allegory and legend. The 85-m (279-ft) tower (Monday to Friday 9am–7pm, Saturday, Sunday, public holidays 10am–7pm;

admission charge) dominates the scene. It contains the fourth largest ★ **Glockenspiel** (carillon) in Europe, which is a popular attraction for visitors. Forty-three bells covering 3½ octaves play four different tunes (daily at 11am, noon and 5pm).

The Glockenspiel

While the music is playing, two scenes with moving figures are portrayed: a remembrance of the tournament at the m_____ _____ ___ _____ Wilhelm V and Renate _____ re-minder ____ _____ ____ ____ ____ _ich gave th_ ____ ____ ____ ____ ___ All year ro__ ____ ____ ____ ____ ___ hen the Mü_ ____ ____ ____ ____ midt in 190_ ____ ____ ____ ____ ight-watch_ ____ ____ ____ ____ al.

In f_____ ____ ____ ____ ___ **lumn** (Mari____ ____ ____ ____ ___ 1638 at Schrannenplatz ___ _ ____ ____ ___ of the cities of Munich and Landshut from the ravages of the Thirty Years War. A monolith of red Tegernsee marble bears the 2.15-m (7-ft) high Madonna figure. The gilded statue with sceptre and crown stands on a crescent moon, along with the Christ child delivering a blessing. It is a work by Herbert Gerhard (1594) which graced the high altar of the Frauenkirche until 1620. Four early baroque *putti*, symbolically fighting against the curses of mankind (plague, war, hunger and heresy), are decorations at the base of the column. The bronzes were probably made by Jörg Petel from Weilheim.

The Fish Fountain

The **Fish Fountain** (Fischbrunnen) in the northeast corner of the square was erected in 1862–5 by Konrad Knoll; it suffered severe damage in 1944 and was built anew in 1954 by Josef Henselmann, who used some of the original bronze parts that had been saved.

The east side of Marienplatz is bounded by the **Old Town Hall** (Altes Rathaus). The present building was erected in 1953–8; it is however based on the Gothic model destroyed during the war, which had been designed by Jörg von Halspach, architect of the Frauenkirche, and built in 1474. In former times the Gothic hall served mainly for dancing. It was considered the most perfect late-Gothic secular hall in southern Germany. It has been restored in greatly simplified form. Erasmus Grasser created the sequence of 16 *Moriskentänzer* (Morris Dancers), of which, unfortunately, only ten have been preserved. Today the originals are on display in the Munich Stadtmuseum (*see page 21*). The former Talbrucktor (gateway), which had already been converted to the town hall tower in the Gothic period, was rebuilt in 1972 by Erwin Schleich according to the Gothic original. The tower houses the Munich Toy Museum.

St Peter's Church

Route 2

The Burghers' Munich: Church of St Peter – Asam Church – Sendlinger Tor – City Museum – Viktualienmarkt – Church of the Holy Ghost

This walk can be undertaken as a continuation of Route 1. Without a visit to the Stadtmuseum it takes about 1½ hours. Leaving Marienplatz you follow the Rindermarkt to the ★ **Church of St Peter** ❽, the oldest parish church in Munich. Even prior to the founding of the city by Henry the Lion, there had been a church from pre-Merovingian times on this site. This fact was revealed by excavations carried out between 1952–3. Towards the end of the 12th century the second church in Bavarian Romanesque style was consecrated. After the church building had been expanded in Gothic style by order of the bishop of Freising, and consecrated in 1294, it fell victim to the great fire of 1327. After reconstruction St Peter's was dedicated anew in 1368.

The 92-m (302-ft) ★ **spire**, built anew in 1607 and rebuilt according to the original after the war, is regarded as one of Munich's landmarks. From its platform there is a magnificent ★ **view of the city** and, during periods of *Föhn* weather, of the Alps (Monday to Saturday 9am–6pm, Sunday and public holidays 10am–1pm; admission charge).

Many of the interior furnishings were preserved in World War II. Most important was the rescue of the ★ **high altar**, to which Erasmus Grasser had contributed a seated figure of St Peter (1492), Egid Quirin Asam the Four Fathers of the Church (1732) and Franz Schwanthaler two worshipping angels (1804). The figure of Christ and the

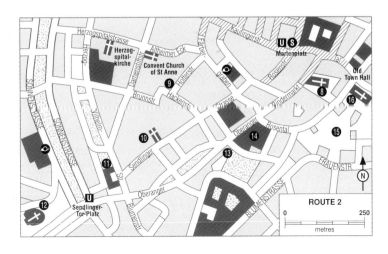

statue of Mary on the right and left side of the altar are the work of Joseph Prötzner the Elder. The ★ **five Gothic pictures of St Peter** by Jan Polack (1517), which used to be part of the high altar, are now on the walls of the presbytery. Of further interest are the Shrenck Altarpiece, a rare sandstone retable of about 1400 with a depiction of the *Last Judgement*, in the north aisle, the Corpus Christi Altar by Ignaz Günther (1758) on the front of the northern aisle, and the Aresing Epitaph by Erasmus Grasser (1482) in the chapel under the north tower. The St Eligius Altar is by Ignaz Günther as well (1770). The same artist created the Epitaph of TE de Courcelles above the chapel of the south tower. The exquisite baptismal font in the chapel was made by Hans Krumper in 1620. In the middle of the southern aisle is the St John's Altar by Ignaz Günther (1756). The figures of the Apostles on the pillars in the nave are the work of Faistenberger (St Andrew), Greiff (St Paul) and Joseph Prötzner, who was also responsible for the pulpit.

An Apostle figure

Further on in the direction of Sendlinger Strasse, Rindermarkt street widens into a square, at whose centre is the Rinderbrunnen (cattle fountain), designed by Joseph Henselmann. To get to the old quarter of the city known as the **Altes Hackenviertel ⑨**, you now turn into Färbergraben and approach it by way of Altheimer Eck the Herzogspitalstrasse, with its old Munich buildings: Weinhaus Neuner at No 8 and the Former **Gregorian Seminary** at No 12, which was founded by Albrecht V in 1574 as a student dormitory; the present empire facade dates from the year 1808. In the church of St Elisabeth at No 9, the wooden sculpture of Our Lady of Sorrows by T Pader (1651) is of interest.

19

Now proceed along Damenstiftstrasse. The **Convent Church of St Anne** (Damenstiftstrasse 1) was erected by the brothers Gunezrhainer in 1733 under Elector Karl Albrecht; the Asam brothers were responsible for the stucco and frescoes of the interior, which had to be rebuilt and restored after its destruction in World War II. Connected to the church is the former convent, which, having become a religious foundation for aristocratic ladies (*Damenstift*) in 1784, was converted one year later into the neoclassical style by Matthias Widmann. It is now used as a school.

Turning left into Brunnstrasse you come to Hackenstrasse, where the **Radspielerhaus** (No 7) with its neoclassical facade (Jean-Baptiste Metivier, 1817) is worth seeing. The poet Heinrich Heine dwelt here in 1827–8. Just opposite at No 10 lived the sculptor Johann Baptist Straub, for whom the rococo house was erected in 1741. There is a relief above the portal showing six dogs playing with a ball which presumably gave the house its name

The Radspielerhaus

Altes Hackerhaus

Asamkirche interior

of *Hundskugel* (dog's ball). Zur Hundskugel is also the name of Munich's oldest restaurant (1440), located on the corner of Hotterstrasse.

Continuing on your way down Hackenstrasse and turning right into Sendlinger Strasse, you cannot fail to notice a corner building on the left-hand side. It is the Altes Hackerhaus. The historic home with its Silbersalon (Silver Drawing Room, 1885) can be viewed on Saturday 1–5pm, Sunday 10am–5pm.

Amidst the shops in Sendlinger Strasse rises the famous ★★ **Church of St John Nepomuk** ❿ on the right-hand side (No 62). The church is better known as the Asamkirche, since Egid Quirin Asam (1692–1750) wanted to build his own private church here. Although Asam had taken over all the costs for the construction of the building, he was forced to make it accessible to the public after fierce resistance on the part of the citizens. In 1733 the foundation stone was laid, and the consecration took place in 1746. Asam was assisted by his brother Cosmas Damian in designing the church, which is one of the most splendid achievements of Bavarian rococo.

The deeds of St John Nepomuk are depicted on the ornate facade. The interior seems a cross between a lavish theatre auditorium and a mystic grotto. With a gallery running round it on all sides, the high, narrow nave ends at the two-tiered high altar, above which is Egid Quirin's ★ *Throne of Mercy*, the crucified Christ held in the arms of God. The Asamkirche is framed by the Priest's House (1771) on the right and the **Asamhaus** on the left, which was bought by Egid Quirin Asam in 1733. The Asamhof to the back of the church is a modern shopping and residential quarter.

At the end of the street is the **Sendlinger Tor** ⓫. This gateway was erected in 1318, when Ludwig the Bavarian expanded the city and had a second ring of walls built. Of the original fortification only the two hexagonal flanking towers remain. Across Sendlinger-Tor-Platz you can see the distinctive Protestant **Church of St Matthew** ⓬, designed in 1953–5 by Gustav Gsaenger.

The route leads back to Oberanger, a street parallel to Sendlinger Strasse. At No 11 is the **Ignaz-Günther-Haus** ⓭, which the famous rococo sculptor acquired in 1761 as a dwelling and workshop. This edifice of Gothic origin was restored in 1977. On the ground floor there is an exhibition about the life and work of the artist.

Between St-Jakobs-Platz, Oberanger and Rosental you find the **Munich City Museum** ⓮ (Stadtmuseum). The original edifice, which served as the city arsenal, was built in Gothic style towards the end of the 15th century. Only the vaulted hall on the ground floor survived the war, and restoration wasn't completed until 1978.

Today the museum Moriskenraum, a room the ★ **Moriskentänze** Grasser (1480), and al hall of armour. The se including an enlarge (1572) and the photogr floor. In addition, spe played on this floor. C rooms with original f

rris Dancers

A vast ★ **Puppet Theatre Collection,** with ...

uppet Theatre Collection

all continents and almost all periods, is located on the third floor. The extensive musical instrument collection is kept on the fourth floor.

Passing through Rosental in an easterly direction, you come to the ★ **Viktualienmarkt ⑮**. Selling an extraordinary variety of fresh produce, this bustling open-air market is considered the popular centre of the city. Munich's six most popular folksingers and comedians have statues commemorating them here, designed by different artists. The fountain figures represent the unique Karl Valentin (1882–1948) and his partner Liesl Karlstadt (1892–1960), the comedian Weiss Ferdl (1883–1949), the couplet singer Roider Jackl (1906–75), Elise Aulinger (1881–1965) and Ida Schumacher (1895–1956).

21

The **Church of the Holy Ghost ⑯** (Heiliggeistkirche) looks down upon the Viktualienmarkt from the north. It is one of the oldest churches in Munich. In the early 13th century Duke Ludwig I had a hospital and a chapel built on this site, but in 1327 these were completely destroyed by the great fire. The Gothic hall church and connecting hospital were finished in 1392 and in 1724–30 the church's interior was completely renovated in baroque style by Johann Georg Ettenhofer and the Asam brothers.

Wooden sculpture in the Church of the Holy Ghost

The high altar (1727) by Nikolaus Stuber was destroyed in World War II, but has been restored. It has a painting by Ulrich Loth (1644); the ★ **angel figures** (about 1730) are originals by Johann Georg Greiff. To the right of the high altar stands the John the Baptist Altar by Antonio Matteo (1730), the painting *The Baptism of Christ* is the work of Melchior Steidl (1720). The church's main treasure, the *Hammerthal Madonna* (1450), was saved from destruction in the war and now stands on the Lady altar in the middle of the north wall. Exactly opposite in the Kreuzkapelle (Chapel of the Cross), constructed in 1907, a late-Gothic cross (1501) on the south wall is of special interest. Beneath the west gallery the bronze tomb of Duke Ferdinand of Bavaria, designed by Hans Krumper in 1588, can be seen. The vault frescoes by the Asam brothers were destroyed in the war, but were completely restored by Karl Manninger.

The Hofbräuhaus

Route 3

Medieval Munich: Marienplatz – Burgstrasse – Alter Hof – Central Mint – Post Office No 1 – Hofbräuhaus – Isartor – Deutsches Museum

This walk leads through medieval Munich. Its narrow little lanes still retain a strongly medieval character. The route through the old town – without a visit to the Deutsches Museum – takes about one hour and is a continuation of Route 2.

From Marienplatz (or the Heiliggeistkirche) turning immediately in front of the main facade of the Old Town Hall, you come to **Burgstrasse**. This street runs along the northeastern edge of what was formerly the oldest town wall. The slight slope down to where the moat used to be (a branch of the Isar), can still be seen.

House No 5 used to be (as of 1550) the City Scriveners' Office. It is the only fully preserved late-Gothic building in Munich. With its vaulted rooms, arcaded courtyard, spiral tower and 'Jacob's Ladder' staircase, as well as its facade, it is a prime example of secular architecture

The Weinstadl

Mozart lived here

from this period. Today the building houses the *Weinstadl*, a very popular tavern. In the adjacent house, **No 7**, the composer Wolfgang Amadeus Mozart had a temporary abode while composing the opera *Idomeneo*, which was first performed in Munich in 1781. In **house No 8** the court architect François de Cuvilliés, designer of the Amalienburg and the Alte Residenz, died. **No 6** was the lifetime residence of Wiguläus Freiherr von Kreittmayr (1705–90), who was an important Bavarian legislator.

A short detour through the Schlichtinger-Bogen (archway) leads via Ledererstrasse to the **Zerwirkgewölbe**, an elegant Renaissance building, where even today game and poultry are prepared and sold. In 1591 the very first Hofbräuhaus was built here. In medieval times Ludwig the Stern (1264) had his falconry here.

Burgstrasse leads to the archway of the old royal residence, the **Alter Hof** . Ludwig the Stern (1253–94), having chosen Munich as his place of residence after the first partition of Bavaria, had it built in the then northeastern part of the city in 1255. Ludwig the Bavarian (1294–1347), elected German emperor in 1328, made the building his imperial residence and kept the imperial insignia in the St Laurence chapel (no longer in existence), which formed the northern part of the Alter Hof. The late-Gothic west wing has been preserved, in spite of later alterations and severe damage to the whole complex in World War II. Since the restoration work in 1968 the Alter Hof has again acquired much of its medieval form. Even a reconstruction of the facade painting on the little oriel turret adorning the south wing has been faithful to the original design.

The Alter Hof

The Wittelsbachs – with the exception of Sigismund, who continued to use the Alter Hof as his residence when in Munich – saw themselves compelled by civil upheaval to order the construction of a new residence, the so-called New Palace on the edge of the city expanded by Ludwig the Bavarian. As a consequence of this the Alter Hof became a mainly administrative building. Since 1816 it has housed the fiscal offices of the city.

Probably in order to have a connection between the Alter Hof and the new residence, in 1563 Duke Albrecht V (1550–79) commissioned his court architect Wilhelm Egkl to erect the royal stables. From the 19th century until 1986 the building served as the **Central Mint** 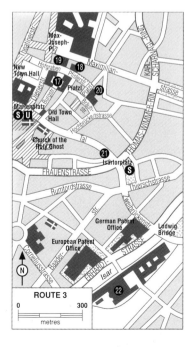 (Bayerisches Hauptmünzamt). On the ground floor were the stables, on the upper storey the cabinet of curiosities as well as the library. The former stable building is of particular interest on account of its inner courtyard, the ★ **Münzhof**. Divided into three storeys, each with glorious leaf-formed arcades, this courtyard is a superb example of Bavarian Renaissance style.

In the 19th century the mint was given new facades. The wall facing the town moat was done in early neoclassical style by Andreas Gärtner and Franz Thurn in 1809. The

23

facade facing Maximilianstrasse was designed in 1859–63 by Friedrich Bürklein. It was meant to blend in with the general architectural concept of the street.

Passing from the former mint (now the Bavarian State Office for the Preservation of Historical Monuments) through Hofgraben to Maximilianstrasse, you turn left and after a few steps reach **Post Office No 1 ⑲**. This palace used to belong to the counts of Törring-Jettenbach, who commissioned the brothers Gunezrhainer to build it in 1747–54. In 1834 Leo von Klenze transformed the building into the central post office. In 1836 Klenze designed the arcade on the north side to provide an appropriate finishing touch to Max-Joseph-Platz with the Residence and the National Theatre. The frescoes in the arcade are called the horse-tamers, and are the work of Johann Georg Hiltensperger.

The building, damaged during the war, was rebuilt in 1952–3. The baroque entrance, which survived the war, has been incorporated into the main hall. Some of Johann Baptist Straub's figures (1772) have been placed in the lobby and some in the Bavarian National Museum. They used to adorn the staircase hall.

A venerable institution

Walking back to Hofgraben you go through the Pfisterbogen and Pfisterstrasse to reach a famous tourist attraction, much praised in song, the ★ **Hofbräuhaus ⑳**. Originally the ducal, then the royal, and since 1852 the state brewery, it has been in existence since 1589. The present building was designed by Littmann and Maxon in 1896–7, and the concept was influenced by old Munich town houses. The tap room on the ground floor has a cheerful atmosphere, with music and plenty of beer and nearly all tourists want to visit it. In the upper floors, however, the Hofbräuhaus is more refined. In the festival hall a brass band plays every evening during the season. On a warm summer evening it is quite pleasant to sit in the inner courtyard with its arcades.

Opposite the Hofbräuhaus is the **Platzl**, an old Munich institution with a Bavarian folklore programme. In the souvenir shops around here, however, you will hardly find any genuine Munich items.

If you walk down Bräuhausstrasse in an easterly direction and turn right into Hochbrückenstrasse, you see on the opposite side, at No 8, the Moradelli House, a typical old Munich 17th-century town house, with a gorgeous courtyard with leaves and balconies around it.

The Isartor

Continuing along Hochbrückenstrasse you reach the Tal. About 200m (656 ft) to the east is the **Isartor ㉑**. This gate was part of the fortifications built by Ludwig the Bavarian after he had expanded the city towards the Isar in 1337. In 1833 Friedrich von Gärtner was entrusted with the restoration of the gate, in the course of which Bernhard Neher painted a fresco on the outside of the main tower in 1835; this work depicts the entry into Munich of Emperor Ludwig the Bavarian after the victorious battle against the Habsburgs at Mühldorf in 1322. Polish specialists were hired for the restoration of the Isartor in 1972.

The Isartor houses the **Karl Valentin Musäum** (*see page 80*), a typically Munich collection of curiosities, dedicated to the popular comedian Karl Valentin.

From Isartorplatz the walk continues in an easterly direction towards the Isar, to the site where Henry the Lion had the first wooden bridge built, which led to the development of Munich. The present Ludwigsbrücke was built in 1934–5.

North of the bridge, to the left, is the **Volksbad** (public baths) built by Carl Hocheder from 1897–1901, and commissioned by Karl Müller. Its art nouveau design and decor is quite unique. Above the river to the east is the imposing **Kulturzentrum am Gasteig** (cultural centre) which opened in 1985. It includes concert and lecture halls, theatres, libraries, the Richard Strauss Conservatory, and is the home of the Munich Philharmonic Orchestra and of the Volkshochschule (adult education centre).

To the right of the bridge, on the island in the Isar, is the new Forum der Technik (Forum of Technology), housed in the former Congress Hall, which has exhibition and conference rooms and an IMAX projection theatre with hourly film presentations. Behind is the huge complex of the ★★★ **Deutsches Museum** . In 1903 Oskar von Miller (1855–1934) founded the Museum of Masterworks of Science and Technology. As a result of Miller's initiative this technical museum came into existence and over the years became the largest of its kind in the world. The foundation stone of the main building was laid in 1906 in the presence of Emperor Wilhelm II.

Gabriel von Seidl won the first prize in a competition for his plans. After his death in 1914 his brother Emanuel continued with the project, and the museum was finally opened in 1925. From 1928 to 1935 additional buildings, the library and former congress hall, were designed by German Bestelmeier. During World War II, 80 percent of the museum was severely damaged and 20 percent of the exhibits were completely destroyed. In its present reconstructed state the museum comprises an exhibition area of 55,000sq m (65,779sq yds). Adjacent to the museum is a library housing about 720,000 volumes. A branch of the Deutsches Museum, the Flugwerft Schleissheim (aircraft hangar), was opened in the immediate vicinity of the Oberschleissheim palaces (*see page 73*). It comprises the restored Historic Hangar, built between 1912 and 1919, a restoration workshop and an exhibition

Eccentric opening times at the Karl Valentin Musäum

25

The Deutsches Museum

hall. The Museum, Library and Schleissheim Branch are open daily 9am–5pm except on New Year's Day, Shrove Tuesday, Good Friday, Easter Sunday, 1 May , Whit Sunday, Corpus Christi, 1 November, 24, 25, 31 December, and from 2pm on the second Wednesday in December; admission charge.

The individual departments are:

Down the mine

Ground floor and basement
1 Mineral resources (with illustrative material on the history of the earth and the evolution of life).
2 Open-cast mining.
2A Mineral gas, mineral oil.
3 Mining (mining techniques, salt-mines, coal mines).
3A Modern mining.
4 Mineral dressing.
5 Machine tools.
6 Testing of materials; welding and soldering.
7 Engines (muscle-power machines, wind-powered generators, hydraulic machines; internal-combustion engines; steam, water and gas powered turbines).
8 Land transport (walking aids, sledges and carriages; motor-cars; bicycles and motor bicycles; railways).
9 Motor vehicles.
10 Model railway.
11 Open-air collection (cranes, windmill, lifeboat).
12 Tunnelling, construction of underground railways.
13 Roads and bridges.
14 Hydraulic engineering.
15 Heavy electrical engineering (Faraday Cage) on the ground floor.
16 Marine navigation (evolution of the ship, development of nautical instruments).
17 Aeronautics (from balloons and airships to jet propulsion and rockets).

Amongst the planes

1st floor
18 Scientific instruments.
19 Physics (mechanics of solids, mechanics of liquids and gases; oscillations and waves; heat; electricity, optics).
20 Energetics (nuclear physics, including Otto Hahn's apparatus for nuclear fission).
21 History of the Deutsches Museum.
22 Musical instruments.
23 Scientific Chemistry.
24 Technical Chemistry.

2nd floor
25 Altamira Cave.

26 Glass blowing and ceramics.
27 Glass technology.
28 Technical toys.
29 Paper.
30 Writing and printing.
31 Space travel.
32 Photography.
33 Textile technology.

3rd floor

34 Weights and measures.
35 Time measurement (from sun dial to modern quartz technique).
36 Agriculture (arable farming, dairy, sugar manufacture, brewery).
37 Telecommunications.
38 Information science, automation, microelectronics.
39 Astronomy.

4th to 6th floor

Observatory, amateur radio operations, astronomy, and Planetarium. Several times a day there are demonstrations in the Planetarium. Tickets should be purchased beforehand in the entrance hall.

Textile technology

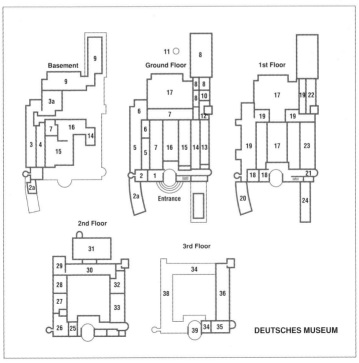

DEUTSCHES MUSEUM

Max-Joseph-Platz

Route 4

Royal Munich: Max-Joseph-Platz – National Theatre – Residenz – Hofgarten – Former Army Museum

This route leads through royal Munich and concentrates on the Residence. If you want to include its museums and theatres, you will need a whole day to see it.

Within five minutes from Marienplatz, Dienerstrasse leads through to ★ **Max-Joseph-Platz** ㉓. The present form of this cobblestone square goes back to Ludwig I (ruled 1825–48). In the centre of the square is the bronze statue of Maximilian I Joseph, erected in his memory by his son Ludwig I. The monument was designed by the Berlin sculptor Christian Daniel Rauch in 1832 and cast by JB Stiglmaier. It was unveiled in 1835.

Behind the monument rises the neoclassical facade of the ★ **National Theatre** ㉔. Up to 1803 there was a Franciscan monastery on this site, which was pulled down in the course of secularisation. Since the citizens of Munich had been demanding an opera house for some time (the Old Residence Theatre was reserved for the royal court), Maximilian I Joseph announced an architectural competition among the great architects of his time. To everyone's surprise this royal competition was won by a 21-year-old newcomer named Carl von Fischer. In 1811 construction began, with Crown Prince Ludwig laying the foundation stone. Completed in 1818, the building burnt down in 1823, but was rebuilt according to the original plans by Leo von Klenze in 1825. In 1943 the theatre was almost completely destroyed by bombs. Its reconstruction in 1963, true to the original plans, even down to the decoration of the rooms, cost 63 million marks. Only in the lower pediment were the original plans disregarded. The sculptor Georg Brenninger was commissioned to create a monumental group *Apollo and the Muses*, which was placed there in 1972. Further renovations were carried out at the end of the 1980s and early 1990s, including the instalment of what was at the time the most modern stage machinery in Europe.

To the left of the National Theatre is the modern **Residence Theatre** ㉕, which was built in 1948–51 by Karl Hocheder in place of the Cuvilliés Theatre (*see page 30*).

The Residence Theatre

The south side of Max-Joseph-Platz is taken up by the building of Post Office No 1 (*see page 24*), the arcade of which was designed by Klenze. The west side is adorned by some town houses in Munich style, one of which, Residenzstrasse 13 ㉖, deserves special mention. The **Eilles Court**, as it is known, has the only traditional Renaissance courtyard still existing in Munich, built about 1560 and renovated in 1971. The three-storey ★ **arcaded courtyard** is structured with colonnades and pierced brickwork balustrades.

The northern end of the square is formed by the Royal Palace of the Residence (*see page 31*), and the entrance to the museum of the Residence and the Treasury is here.

The main entrance to the ★ **Residenz** ㉗ is located in the narrow Residenzstrasse. Because of the rapid growth of the city as well as popular uprisings, in 1385 the Wittelsbachs felt forced to give up their residence, the Alter Hof,

The Residenz

29

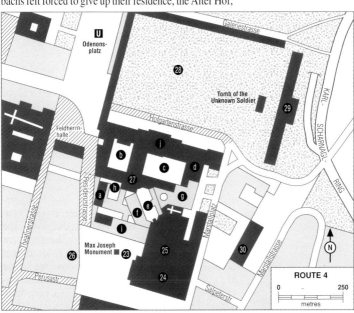

ROUTE 4
0   250
metres

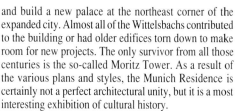

and build a new palace at the northeast corner of the expanded city. Almost all of the Wittelsbachs contributed to the building or had older edifices torn down to make room for new projects. The only survivor from all those centuries is the so-called Moritz Tower. As a result of the various plans and styles, the Munich Residence is certainly not a perfect architectural unity, but it is a most interesting exhibition of cultural history.

The **Maximilian Residenz [a]** extends along Residenz-strasse (*see Map on page 29*). It was erected between 1611 and 1619 by Hans Krumper and Heinrich Schön. After World War II its original Renaissance facade was restored. In a raised niche between the portals stands the *Patrona Boiariae*, a bronze statue of the Virgin created by Hans Krumper in 1616. This figure, which was commissioned by Elector Maximilian I, actually became the Bavarian patron saint. Krumper also designed the Allegories of the four cardinal virtues, which decorate the slanting gables of the marble portals. The lions, two in front of each entrance, are the work of Hubert Gerhard.

The Patrona Boiariae

The left portal leads to the **Kaiserhof** or Emperor's Court **[b]**, the facade of which was created anew by Hermann Kaspar. This open square joins the **Apothek-enhof** or Apothecary Court **[c]** to the east, which was built under Maximilian I. It was restored, however, in the later style it had been given by Ludwig I. From 1832 to 1842 Leo von Klenze worked on the festival hall (*see page 34*) to the left, which has a terrace and an outside staircase towards the Apothekenhof. To the east, in the so-called Apothekenflügel or wing **[d]**, are the rooms of the Academy of Sciences.

The Brunnenhof

In the south (to the right) is the ★ **Brunnenhof** or Fountain Court **[e]**, the earliest edifice of which is the ★ **Antiquarium [f]** (*see page 32*), built in 1571 under Albrecht V. Maximilian I commissioned Hans Krumper to complete this courtyard in the form of a long, stretched octagon (1610–20, restored in 1958). The centre is dominated by the ★ **Wittelsbach fountain**, for which Hubert Gerhard designed the bronze figures between 1611–14. At the feet of Duke Otto von Wittelsbach are four mermen symbolising the four most important Bavarian rivers. The fountain is embellished with gods, animals and *putti* (cherubs).

The Cuvilliés Theatre

From the Brunnenhof you enter the ★★ **Altes Residenz-theater** or Old Residence Theatre **[g]**, which is world famous under the name of its designer as the Cuvilliés Theatre. This masterpiece of rococo style was originally located where the present Residenztheater stands. Elector Maximilian III Joseph had it constructed outside the Residenz in 1751 after a fire had reduced the original theatre in the palace to ashes. The Cuvilliés Theatre found its present location after the war, when the destroyed Brunnenhof layout was reconstructed. Because the ★★**interior decorations** were put into safekeeping during the war, the original majesty of this rococo jewel, created by François de Cuvilliés (1731–77), can be admired once more (Monday to Saturday 2–5pm, Sunday and public holidays 10am–5pm; admission charge).

Leave the Brunnenhof at the western corner to enter the **Kapellenhof** or Chapel Court [**h**], where you pass the entrance of the Staatliche Münzsammlung or State Coin Collection. The Kapellenhof leads back to Residenzstrasse, which runs into Max-Joseph-Platz on the left.

The ★**Königsbau** or King's Tract [**i**], bordering the square on the north side, was built in 1826–35 at the command of Ludwig I. The architect was Leo von Klenze, who, applying designs of Carl von Fischer, expanded the facade to include 21 bays. The three-storey middle section was patterned on the Palazzo Pitti in Florence. The facade is of sandstone with heavy diamond-patterned rustication so typical of the High Renaissance. The King's Tract housed the apartments of Ludwig I.

In the Residence Museum

The central portal is the entrance to the ★**Residence Museum**. On the right-hand side of the hall is the entrance to the ★**Schatzkammer** or Treasury, one of the most important collections of ecclesiastical and secular treasures in Europe, including crowns and gems, goldsmiths' work and jewels from ten centuries. It is located in rooms **I–X** and must be visited separately. The numbers given below follow the official numbering of the rooms in the Residence Museum. A viewing of rooms **1–81** is recommended for a morning tour; rooms **82–112** can then be seen in the afternoon.

Priceless treasures

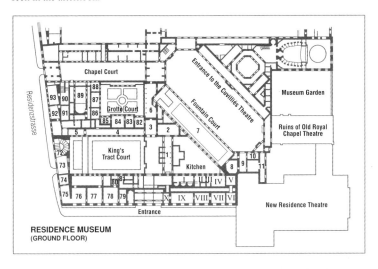

RESIDENCE MUSEUM
(GROUND FLOOR)

Entering the Grotto Court

Perseus

33–41 Former Court Garden rooms, designed in 1612
by Charles Puille and expanded to house Princess
Charlotte in 1814

42 Charlotte Passage

Residenz m. State Collection of Egyptian Art. (handwritten)

43–44 Vestibule and Bro

45 Vestibule to Hall

46–53 Emperor's Tract
dating from 161
Chamber, Confer
Candid.

54 Hall of Knights c

55–62 ★★ **Ornate Room**
inal rooms, designed by Joseph Effner for Elector Karl Albrecht in 1726, were destroyed by fire
in 1729. François de Cuvilliés converted them
into masterpieces of rococo, with the aid of Johann
Baptist Zimmermann, who did the stucco-work.

63 Chinese Cabinet.

64–65 Cloakroom and passageway.

66–71 ★ **Papal Rooms**, so named because Pope Pius VI
lived in them in 1782. These elegant baroque
rooms were designed by Agostino Barelli in
1665–7; they include the ★ Cabinet of the Heart,
with baroque allegories of love.

72 Queen Mother's Staircase.

73 Passage to King's Tract.

74 Anteroom.

75–79 Nibelung Halls designed by Leo von Klenze in
1827–34 for Ludwig I; the paintings of the Nibelung saga are by Julius Schnorr von Carolsfeld.

80–81 Passageway and staircase to the King's Tract.

Rooms

33

RESIDENCE MUSEUM
(FIRST FLOOR)

Residenzstrasse

Chapel Court
Grotto Court
Fountain Court
Museum Garden
Ruins of Old Royal Chapel Theatre
King's Tract Court
Kitchen
14 Royal Apartments
New Residence Theatre

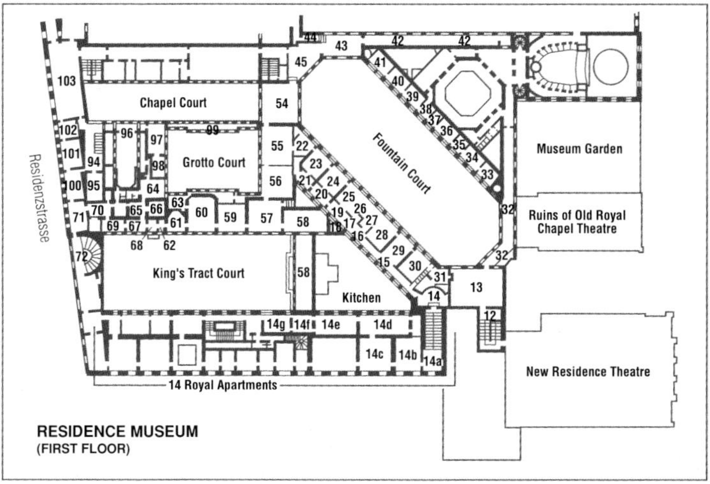

On the afternoon tour, go through rooms 1–3 to reach:

82–88 Yellow Rooms, designed by Cuvilliés the Elder about 1730 and today containing a collection of 18th-century European porcelain.

89 Court chapel (built 1601–3).

90 Lower landing of chapel staircase.

91–93 Vestment rooms (ecclesiastical vestments).

94 Chapel staircase.

95 Reliquary chamber.

96 Gallery of the court chapel.

97–98 Anteroom and Ornate Chapel, the private chapel of Maximilian I, designed by Hans Krumper.

99 Antler Passage.

100–2 Silver rooms.

103 Hartschier Room.

104–9 Stone rooms, constructed between 1612 and 1617 to a general design by Hans Krumper. Maximilian I had all these rooms painted; some of the work was by Peter Candid and Johann Anton Gumpp.

110–12 Room of the Four Grays, Emperor's Room, Emperor's Staircase.

The north tract **[j]** of the Residenz, the facade of which was constructed by Leo von Klenze for Ludwig I, adjoins the **State Collection of Egyptian Art**, one of the finest collections of its kind in the world. On the first floor is the **Festsaalbau** or Festival Hall. Today it is used for concerts and is known as the Herkulessaal (after its tapestries which have scenes from the Hercules legend).

In the Hofgarten

Opposite the north tract is the ★ **Hofgarten ㉘** or Court Garden, which was laid out at the time of Maximilian I. In the middle of this French-style park stands a circular temple, probably the work of Heinrich Schön (1615). Its roof is crowned by a copy of the Bavaria statue modelled by Herbert Gerhard in 1594.

The temple

The Hofgarten arcades, including the gateway designed by Klenze, were restored in 1950. The frescoes in the arcades were by Wilhelm von Kaulbach. In the northern wing are the rooms of the Kunstverein (society of arts), private galleries, and the Theatre Museum. The Tomb of the Unknown Soldier at the east end of the Hofgarten was constructed by Bernhard Bleeker in 1924.

The Hofgarten Café

Behind the tomb towers the cupola of the former Armeemuseum or **Army Museum ㉙**. This building has now been integrated into the new and highly controversial Bavarian State Chancellery. To the south is Marstallplatz, on the left side of which is the former **Royal Riding School ㉚** and stables. Built in 1817–22, this neoclassical building is used for the experimental stage of the Theater im Marstall. Further south comes Maximilianstrasse; by turning right you arrive back at Max-Joseph-Platz.

Route 5

The Munich of Ludwig I: Odeonsplatz – Ludwigstrasse – Siegestor – Schwabing – English Garden

Elegant Ludwigstrasse

This route leads through an extension of the city planned by Maximilian I Joseph, but mainly achieved through the involvement of Crown Prince Ludwig. This part of town is called Maxvorstadt and was built between 1816 and 1852. Beginning at Odeonsplatz (underground station), the route takes approximately two hours.

Ludwig I commissioned the layout of ★ **Odeonsplatz** and the Ludwigstrasse, which begins here. While still crown prince he entrusted the design to Leo von Klenze. In 1827, two years after taking the throne, Ludwig chose Friedrich von Gärtner to supervise the construction.

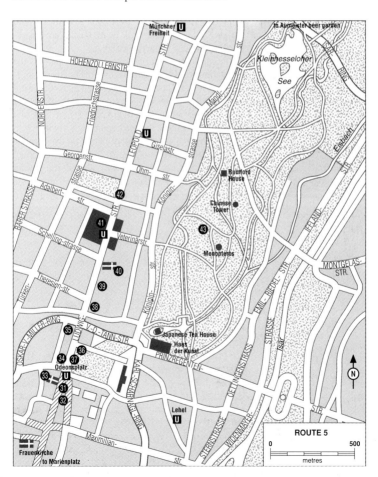

So the **Feldherrnhalle** ❸ or Field Marshals' Hall (erected 1841–4) was the work of Gärtner and not of Klenze, who was responsible for the rest of the neoclassical buildings from Odeonsplatz to Theresienstrasse. The model for this hall was the Loggia dei Lanzi in Florence.

Count Tilly

In the left arch stands the bronze figure of Count Tilly, the Bavarian commander during the Thirty Years War; his counterpart on the other side is Prince Wrede, who fought against the French in 1814. Both of these figures were cast by Ferdinand von Miller, according to sketches by Ludwig Schwanthaler. The memorial on the rear wall commemorating the victory of the Bavarian army in the war of 1870–1 is also the work of Miller. It was in front of the Feldherrnhalle that Hitler's march through Munich during his attempted putsch of 1923 was brought to a halt.

The Feldherrnhalle backs on to the **Preysing-Palais** ❸ in Residenzstrasse. Joseph Effner was commissioned to build this rococo palace by Count Maximilian von Preysing in 1723–8. The walls on the outside are embellished with stucco in the rococo style.

The Theatine Church

The most prominent edifice on Odeonsplatz is the ★ **Theatinerkirche** ❸. The founding of Theatine Church, dedicated to St Cajetan, is related to a religious oath sworn by Henriette Adelaide of Savoy, the wife of Elector Ferdinand Maria, in 1659. In gratitude for the birth of a male heir, she wanted to have a court church built, which would also serve as a monastery church for the Theatine monks. After the birth of Crown Prince Max Emanuel (1662), Ferdinand Maria commissioned the Italian architect Agostino Barelli to design a church which would put everything else in the shade. Barelli used the Roman

church St Andrea della Valle as his model. The St Cajetan Church introduced the baroque style in Munich and was in turn used as a model for later sacred structures built by Bavarian electors.

After Barelli had fallen into disfavour in 1667, Enrico Zuccalli took over the artistic direction of the project. He came from a family of masons, who had come to Bavaria from the Grisons in Switzerland. Zuccalli decided the shape of the dome and the towers, but the ultimate design for the facade remained undecided for a long time. For this reason, although the Theatinerkirche was consecrated in 1675, it received its final form at the hands of François de Cuvilliés almost a century later, in 1768. While the towers and dome fully comply with the baroque plan envisaged by Zuccalli, the facade by Cuvilliés, which is almost in Empire style, contrasts with the baroque splendour of the church. The four figures of St Maximilian, St Cajetan, St Ferdinand and St Adelheid are the work of Roman Anton Boos.

The interior has its walls and ceiling elaborately decorated with stucco: the Italian influence is clearly to be seen. Wolfgang Leutner created the stucco figures in full relief, while Nicolo Petri was responsible for the decorations (1685–8). The high altar is a copy of the original, which was destroyed. Caspar de Crayer painted the picture *Mary Enthroned* in 1646. In the west wall of the northern transept is the entrance to the royal vault, in which Ferdinand Maria, Max Emanuel, Karl Albrecht, Maximilian III Joseph, Karl Theodor, King Max I, King Otto of Greece and Crown Prince Rupprecht are buried.

Italian baroque in the Theatine Church

In the northern part of the transept stands the Altar of Mary with the painting *The Holy Family* by Carlo Cignani (1676). The *Annunciation* is by George Desmareés, the St Mark statue by Balthasar Ableithner (1672). In the southern part of the transept there is the St Cajetan Altar with the painting *The Intercession of St Cajetan*, created by Joachim Sandrart in 1671. Balthasar Ableithner was responsible for the statue of St John. The great black pulpit is a work of Andreas Faistenberger (1686). *The Descent from the Cross* in the middle southern side chapel was painted by a pupil of Tintoretto.

North of the Theatinerkirche is the Moy-Palais. This was the first neoclassical edifice built in Ludwigstrasse and was the work of Leo von Klenze (1819).

On the north side of Odeonsplatz is the **Odeon** ❸❹. In 1826–8 Ludwig I commissioned Leo von Klenze with the construction of an Academy of Music complete with concert hall. The building was only partially reconstructed after the war; once famous for its acoustics, the old hall is now the interior courtyard. Other parts of the building today house the Bavarian Ministry of the Interior.

The equestrian statue of Ludwig I

Ludwig instructed Klenze to adapt the facade to that of the **Leuchtenberg-Palais** ❸, which Klenze had built in 1816–21 for Eugène de Beauharnais, the stepson of Napoleon, son-in-law of Maximilian I Joseph, and former Viceroy of Italy, who was living in exile in Munich and bore the title of Duke of Leuchtenberg. Klenze supposedly used the Palazzo Farnese in Rome as his model. Today the building serves as the Bavarian Ministry of Finance.

Opposite these last two buildings is the **Basargebäude** ❸, a neoclassical building that Klenze built in 1824–6 to provide a boundary between Odeonsplatz and Hofgarten. The **equestrian statue of Ludwig I** ❸ was dedicated to the king by the city of Munich in 1862. The monument was designed by one of Schwanthaler's brightest pupils, Max von Widenmann.

Continuing north from Odeonsplatz and walking along ★ **Ludwigstrasse** you see on the right-hand side a building erected during the Third Reich, which interrupts the harmony of the street as designed by Leo von Klenze. It now houses the Bavarian Ministry for Food, Agriculture and Forestry. The next major building on the right-hand side of the street, the former **Bayerisches Kriegsministerium** ❸ or Bavarian War Ministry, is the last building Klenze erected in Ludwigstrasse (1824–30). This former ministry, reconstructed in 1966, now houses the Bavarian State Archives and the Institute for Bavarian History.

From this point Friedrich von Gärtner took over the further development of Ludwigstrasse in 1832. After long disputes with Ludwig I, leading three times to a change of plans, Gärtner built the **Bavarian State Library** (Bayerische Staatsbibliothek) ❸ in 1832–9. The building incorporates stylistic elements from the Florentine Palazzo Strozzi. In front of the building there is a flight of steps on either side of the entrance, which is decorated with the statues of Homer, Thucydides, Aristotle, and Hippocrates. The principal point of interest inside the library is the staircase with its monolithic pillars and Corinthian capitals. Opposite the state library there are the buildings of a former Foundation for Ladies and a former Institute for the Blind, both designed by Gärtner in 1840–3.

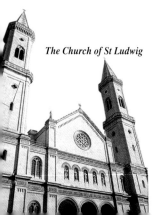

The Church of St Ludwig

The first plans for the construction of the **Parish Church of St Ludwig** ❹ had already been submitted to the king by Leo von Klenze. But he was far from enthralled by the idea of a basilica with low aisles, so he commissioned Friedrich von Gärtner to design a triple-naved basilica; built in 1829–44, it was faithfully reconstructed by Erwin Schleich after its destruction in World War II. The facade, with flanking towers, the cubic rectory (on the left) and Gärtner's former residence (to the right; now the University Construction Office) form a splendid ensemble emphasised by arcades, galleries, and the arches of the vestibule. The statues in the facade niches (Christ and the four Evangelists) are by Ludwig Schwanthaler.

The interior of the church, patterned on Romanesque forms, is dominated by frescoes. The great fresco in the choir, *The Last Judgement*, is the work of Peter Cornelius (1836–40). After Michelangelo's *Last Judgement* in Rome's Sistine Chapel, it is the largest church fresco in the history of art.

At the end of Ludwigstrasse, King Ludwig I envisaged a counterpart to Odeonsplatz, which would be a forum of science. So Gärtner designed a square in 1835–40, flanked on one side by the Georgianum (a seminary for Catholic priests) and on the other side by the **University** ❹. The complex is in neo-Romanesque style and embraces the **Geschwister-Scholl/Professor-Huber-Platz**, named in memory of students Sophie and Hans Scholl and musicologist Kurt Huber, who were leaders of the White Rose resistance group during the Third Reich. They were discovered distributing anti-Nazi leaflets in the neoclassical hall of the university, and were guillotined in 1943. The two symmetrical fountains outside were designed by Gärtner.

Geschwister-Scholl/ Professor-Huber-Platz

39

South of Veterinärstrasse stands the aforementioned **Georgianum**. It was built by Gärtner in 1835–9. Further north is the former Max Joseph Foundation, a boarding school for young ladies of rank which was founded by Maximilian I Joseph in 1809 and is now an integral part of the university.

Ludwigstrasse ends at the **Siegestor** ❷ or Triumphal Arch, which was erected on the orders of Ludwig I to commemorate the achievements of the Bavarian Army in the Wars of Liberation of 1814–15. Modelled on the Arch of Constantine in Rome, the Siegestor was begun in 1844 by Gärtner and completed by Eduard Metzger in 1852. The words of Wilhelm Hausenstein added more recently read: 'Dedicated to victory, destroyed by war, an exhortation to peace.' In 1972 the Quadriga, which had collapsed due to damage to the arch, was put back in its original place.

The Siegestor

West of the Siegestor is the Academy of Fine Arts, built by Gottfried Neureuther in Venetian Renaissance style (1874–87). Many of the most famous names in German art have been involved with this establishment at some time or other, including avant-garde artists such as Klee and Kandinsky.

North of the Siegestor begins the famous district of Schwabing, with its main shopping street and promenade, the Leopoldstrasse. This is where Munich's 'beautiful people' meet in the cafés and ice-cream parlours. Fast-food outlets and clip-joints have commercialised this popular

A Schwabing café

The Monopteros

The Chinese Tower

boulevard, where people go to see and to be seen. But the more idyllic, older part of Schwabing can be discovered easily in the side roads that lead off to the English Garden – Werneckstrasse, for example, or Nikolaiplatz. Ainmillerstrasse, on the west side of Leopoldstrasse, was home to a number of turn-of-the-century painters and writers who played a major part in establishing Schwabing's legendary reputation as the artists' quarter of Munich. Both Ainmillerstrasse and Hohenzollernstrasse – Schwabing's foremost shopping street with its boutiques and arcades – have some magnificent *Jugendstil* (art nouveau) facades.

Returning to the university and then going down the narrow Veterinärstrasse, you come to the ★★ **English Garden ⑬**. The park was laid out in the meadows of the Isar under Elector Karl Theodor in 1789 according to plans drawn up by the American Benjamin Thompson, better known as Count Rumford (1753–1814). The garden was developed from 1804 onwards by the landscape gardener Ludwig von Sckell. The English Garden acquired its name because of its informal, so called English style, and is one of Europe's largest city parks.The route leads straight into the park from Veterinärstrasse. After crossing the Eisbach (ice brook), you can't fail to see the **Monopteros** straight ahead, a circular, neoclassical building in the style of a Roman temple with Ionic capitals. Ludwig I commissioned Leo von Klenze to build it in 1837–8 as a memorial to Elector Karl Theodor. The Monopteros provides a marvellous view of the park.

From this circular temple continue north to reach the **Chinese Tower**, which was modelled on the outlook tower in Kew Gardens and built in 1790–1 by Joseph Frey. It burnt down in World War II, but was reconstructed in 1952 according to the original plans. The beer garden surrounding the tower is a popular summer destination for both locals and visitors.

In 1790 Johann Baptist Lechner built the Ökonomiegebäude (economy building, now used as a restaurant), as well as the nearby Rumford House. From this building a path leads due north, crossing a road cutting through the park, to the **Kleinhesseloher See**, an artificial lake laid out in 1799–1812. There are long walks in a northerly direction, eg to the Forsthaus Aumeister (restaurant; 45 minutes) or to the Isar meadows. You can also turn round at the lake and follow a path along the Eisbach leading to the Haus der Kunst (House of Art). Just before this building, which marks the end of the English Garden on the downtown side, there is a **Japanese teahouse**, which was built by Mitsuo Nomura in 1972, on the occasion of the 20th Olympic Summer Games, as Japan's present to the city of Munich. You can return by bus to the inner city.

Wittelsbacherplatz

Route 6

The buildings of the nobility: Odeonsplatz – Wittelsbacherplatz – Archbishop's Palace – Promenadeplatz – Holy Trinity Church – Lenbachplatz – Old Botanical Garden

This walk leads through the former Kreuzviertel and takes about an hour. From Odeonsplatz (U-Bahn connection) go down Brienner Strasse, where after about 100m the spacious ★ **Wittelsbacherplatz** ➍ opens to the right. In the middle of the square stands the equestrian statue of Elector Maximilian I (1597–1651). The rider is the work of Bertel Thorvaldsen, the pedestal was designed by Leo von Klenze.

On the north side of the square is the Ludwig Ferdinand Palais, built by Xaver Widmann in 1822. The facade design is probably the work of Leo von Klenze, who lived in the palace for 25 years. Prince Ludwig Ferdinand moved into the building in 1878.

The route leads westwards from Wittelsbacherplatz along Brienner Strasse to the **Almeida Palace** ➎, erected by Métivier in 1823–4. The elegant neoclassical facade was restored after the war. The adjacent buildings on the right were designed by Leo von Klenze. Turning back and crossing Brienner Strasse you reach Salvatorplatz by way of Amiraplatz. On the left is the building of the **Bavarian Ministry of Culture and Education** ➏. This was formerly part of the Theatine monastery, which was mostly destroyed in World War II. It used to house the monastic library until the secularisation of 1803.

The former **Salvatorkirche** ➐ gave the square its name. The Church of St Saviour was built in 1494 as the chapel for the graveyard of the parish 'to Our Beloved

The Church of St Saviour

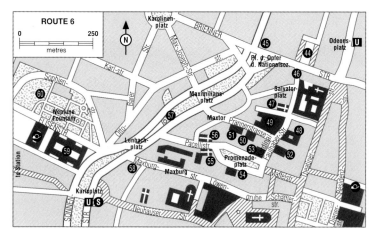

Lady', by Lukas Rottaler, who succeeded Jörg von Halspach (builder of the Frauenkirche) as city architect. The late-Gothic brick church, on whose northern facade remnants of the original frescoes can be seen, has served as a house of worship for the Greek Orthodox Community since 1829.

Salvatorplatz runs into Kardinal-Faulhaber-Strasse.

Detail from the Archbishop's Palace

House No 7 on the left is the ★ **Archbishop's Palace ⑱**. In 1733–7 François de Cuvilliés the Elder built this palace, together with Johann Baptist Zimmermann, for the Count of Holstein, illegitimate son of Elector Karl Albrecht. The building has been the residence of the archbishops of Munich and Freising since 1818.

Across from the Archbishop's Palace in Prannerstrasse, house No 2, the **Palais-Neuhaus-Preysing ⑲**, is equally worth seeing. It is the work of François de Cuvilliés the Elder, who designed a rococo facade here. On the other side of the street at No 7 is the **Palais Seinsheim ⑳**. This noble palace with its rococo facade was probably built about 1760. Next to it, at No 9, is the **Palais Gise ㉑**, which was built about 1760, also in rococo style, by Cuvilliés' pupil Karl Albert von Lespilliez. Only the facade of this building, which was commissioned by Baron von Gise, remains.

Rococo facade

Now turn back to Kardinal-Faulhaber-Strasse and follow it in the direction of Promenadeplatz. On the left-hand side at No 12 is the **Palais Porcia ㉒**. It was built by Enrico Zuccalli in 1693–4 for Count Fugger. In 1731 Elector Karl Albrecht acquired the palace and gave it to his mistress, Countess Morawitzky, later Princess Porcia. It was for her that Cuvilliés redid the facade in rococo style in 1737.

At the corner of Promenadeplatz, at No 2, is the **Palais Montgelas ㉓**. Emanuel Joseph von Herigoyen built it for

Count Montgelas in 1810–11. This neoclassical building is today part of the elegant Bayerischer Hof Hotel. In the pedestrian precinct there is a plaque dedicated to the memory of the socialist leader Kurt Eisner (*see page 9*), who was assassinated on 21 February 1919.

Passing the lawn in the square – statues here commemorate the composer Orlando di Lasso (1532–94), Elector Maximilian Emanuel (1679–1726), the composer Christoph Willibald Gluck (1714–87) and the Bavarian historian Lorenz von Westenrieder (1748–1829) – you come to the **Gunezrhainerhaus** ❺❹. In about 1730 the court architect Johann Baptist Gunezrhainer built this house for himself. On the southwest corner of Promenadeplatz stands the **Carmelite Church** ❺❺. Consecrated in 1660, it is the earliest baroque church in Munich. In 1802–11 Schedel von Greiffenstein created the facade in neoclassical style.

Promenadeplatz turns into Pacellistrasse. On the right is the ★ **Church of the Holy Trinity** ❺❻ (Dreifältigkeitskirche). It was built by Johann Georg Ettenhofer and Enrico Zuccalli in 1711–18 according to the plans of Giovanni Antonio Viscardi. The church was the fulfilment of a vow made by the citizens of Munich during the War of the Spanish Succession. In the pediment niche a bronze figure of St Michael deserves attention.

Altar in the Holy Trinity Church

In the interior of the church, wall-stuccos by Johann Georg Bader (1715) are worth closer inspection. The tambourless cupola has a ceiling fresco by Cosmas Damian Asam (1715). Across from the church you will notice an old clock tower. This is all that remains of the 16th-century fortress built for Albrecht V, which later became the residence of Duke Maximilian Philipp and was called the Maxburg.

Lenbachplatz is separated from Maximiliansplatz by the **Wittelsbach Fountain** ❺❼, designed in 1893–5 by Adolf von Hildebrand. The man slinging a stone and the woman offering a bowl of water symbolise the destructive and healing power of water.

The Wittelsbach Fountain

At the southeast corner of Lenbachplatz is the **Künstlerhaus** ❺❽, the artists' house, built by Gabriel von Seidl in 1893–1900. Nearby, in Herzog-Max-Strasse, is a memorial to the former main synagogue of the Jewish community, built in 1883–7 and demolished in 1938.

West of the Lenbachplatz is the **Palace of Justice** ❺❾. Built by Friedrich von Thiersch, it is one of the most monumental of Munich's late-19th-century buildings. Elements of late-Renaissance are mixed with baroque forms. North of the Palace of Justice is the **Old Botanical Garden** ❻❶, which was laid out by Ludwig von Sckell in 1808–14 as part of the so-called Maxvorstadt suburb.

In the Neue Pinakothek

The door of St Boniface

Route 7

Munich and its museums: Old Botanical Garden – Basilica of St Boniface – Königsplatz – Glyptothek – Collection of Antiquities – Municipal Galleries – Old and New Pinakothek

The Old Botanical Garden (*see page 43*) is within easy reach of Karlsplatz or Lenbachplatz (S-Bahn, U-Bahn and trams). Walk through the park, follow Meiserstrasse, and turn left at Karlsstrasse. On the other side of the street is the **St Boniface Basilica ❺**. Commissioned by Ludwig I, this church was built for the Benedictines by Friedrich Ziebland in 1835–47. The architect had been sent by the king to Rome and Ravenna to study early Christian church architecture. Ziebland erected a basilica with a nave and four aisles, though only half of the nave and the Corinthian portico were restored after the building's partial destruction in World War II. Ludwig I chose the church as the final resting place for himself and his wife Therese. His sarcophagus is in the east aisle and hers is in the crypt.

Returning to Meiserstrasse and following it to the north, you see on the right-hand side of the street the building of the ★ **Graphic Arts Collection ❻** (Staatliche Graphische Sammlung). Prints and drawings from late-Gothic up to present times are on display (*see page 79*). Opposite it is the building of the **Music Academy ❼**. During the Third Reich, the edifice was used as a congress hall. In 1938 the Munich Agreement between Hitler, Chamberlain, Daladier and Mussolini was signed here.

Between the two buildings Brienner Strasse leads to Karolinenplatz. In the middle of the square stands the **Obelisk** commissioned by Ludwig I and designed by Leo von Klenze. The 29-m (95-ft) high monument, with its cladding of twelve iron plates cast from cannons of ships sunk at the Battle of Navarino, was unveiled in 1833. It was built to commemorate the 30,000 Bavarian soldiers who perished in Napoleon's Russian campaign in 1812.

The Obelisk

The route continues westwards to **Königsplatz**. Conceived by Carl von Fischer for Ludwig I, this square was actually laid out by Leo von Klenze. Here Ludwig I wanted to express his predilection for classical Greece. Concreted over and used by the Nazis as a parade ground, the square was only returned to lawn in the 1980s.

On the northern side is the ★ **Glyptothek** . A four-winged complex grouped around a square inner court, it was erected by Leo von Klenze in 1816–30 to house the royal collection of antique sculpture. The neoclassical front was adorned with Ionic columns by Klenze. Above the portico stands a pediment with figures representing Athena surrounded by artists. In the niches of the wings are statues of Hephaestus, Prometheus, Daedalus, Phidias, Pericles and Hadrian.

In the halls of the Glyptothek, which was restored in 1972, exclusively Greek and Roman sculpture from the 6th century BC onwards, is now on display. Of special interest are the Greek statues of youths (room 1), the torso of Apollo by Polycletes (room 2), statues by Praxiteles (room 5) and the ★★ **Aeginates**, two groups of sculptures from the tympanums of the temple of Aphaia at Aegina

The Aeginates

(rooms 7–9). These sculptures, created between 500 and 485BC, depict the combats between Greeks and Trojans and were acquired by Crown Prince Ludwig in 1812.

The south of Königsplatz is dominated by the ★★ **State Collection of Antiquities** (Staatliche Antikensammlung). Commissioned by Ludwig I, this impressive Exhibition Building for Art and Industry was designed by Georg Friedrich Ziebland in 1838–48 in the style of a Corinthian temple. The statues in the pediment, with Bavaria as Patroness of Arts, were modelled according to plans by Schwanthaler.

Since the completion of restoration work in 1967, the museum has housed a priceless array of antique crafts taken from Ludwig I's collection of vases and from the Royal Antiquarium. Among the many exhibits the ★★ **Attic vases** are especially valuable. Apart from pottery from Crete and Mycenae, terracottas, bronzes and a number of jewellery items are on display.

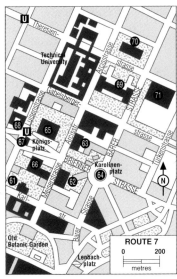

ROUTE 7

0 200

metres

Brienner Strasse is interrupted at Königsplatz by the **Propylaeum** ⑥⑦, which closes the square off to the west. It was commissioned in 1817, but Ludwig I approved Leo von Klenze's design only the day after his abdication on 21 March 1848. The Propylaeum (the Greek word for the entrance to a temple) expresses the close link between Bavaria and Greece. Prince Otto, the second son of Ludwig I, had been crowned king of Greece in 1832. Created by Ludwig Schwanthaler, the sculptures in the pediment and the reliefs on the towers commemorate the Wittelsbach monarch and the Greek wars of independence.

The Municipal Gallery

In Luisenstrasse is the ★★ **Municipal Gallery** (Städtische Galerie) ⑥⑧, also known as the Lenbachhaus, because the painter Franz von Lenbach had this villa built in Florentine Renaissance style by Gabriel von Seidl in 1887. Since 1929 the building has been the property of the city, which uses it to house its collection of paintings. The collection comprises works from the 19th and 20th centuries, including landscape paintings of the Munich School, romantic painters, the famous Gabriele Münter Collection with works by Kandinsky and other artists belonging to the group *Der Blaue Reiter*, and contemporary works of art by Arnulf Rainer, Joseph Beuys, AR Penck and others.

Café for connoisseurs

There is also a considerable collection of prints and drawings, as well as a video archive and photographic collection. The Lenbachhaus has regularly changing exhibitions of contemporary art.

Continue north along Luisenstrasse, then turn right into Gabelsbergerstrasse, and pass the Technical University. Between Arcisstrasse and Barer Strasse, in the middle of a park, is the newly refurbished ★★★ **Alte Pinakothek** ⑥⑨, one of the world's most famous picture galleries. Ludwig I initiated its construction, commissioning Leo von Klenze to work out a plan. The foundation stone was laid in 1826, and the museum was opened in 1836.

The following list briefly mentions the various rooms and departments:

Early Flemish school (rooms I and IIa): among others: Rogier van der Weyden *Adoration of the Magi* and *St Luke painting the Virgin*, Hans Memling *The Seven Joys of Mary*, Lucas van Leyden *Virgin with Donor*.

Early German school (rooms II, IIb, and III): among others: Dürer *Four Apostles* and *Self-portrait in a Fur Coat*, Matthias Grünewald *St Erasmus and Mauritius*, Lucas Cranach the Elder *The Crucified Christ* and Albrecht Altdorfer *Battle of Alexander*.

Italian school (rooms IV and V): among others: Leonardo da Vinci *Madonna and Child*, Raphael

Madonna Tempi and The Holy |
The Annunciation, Botticelli L(
ian The Crown of Thorns and E
The Gonzago Cycle, Veronese   Christ

Flemish school (rooms VI, '
ers: van Dyck Rest during the I
ment, The Honeysuckle Arbor,
of Leukippos, The Drunken Sile
Her Son Frans, The Mass
Bethlehem and Battle of the A

Dutch school (room IX): among others: Rembrandt The
Holy Family, The Sacrificing of Isaac, Representations
from the Passion, Hals Willem van Heythuysen.

Italian baroque school (room X): among others:
Tiepolo Adoration of the Magi, Reni The Assumption.

French school (rooms XI, XIIa, and XII): among
others: Poussin Lamentation of Christ, Claude Lorrain The
Expulsion of Hagar, Fragonard Girl with Dog, Boucher
Marquise de Pompadour.

Venetian school (room XIIb): among others: Guardi
Clock-tower at St Mark's Square.

Spanish school (room VIII): among others: El Greco
The Disrobing of Christ, Murillo Grape and Melon Eaters,
Velázquez Young Spanish Nobleman.

47

Cabinets

1–2 Giotto The Last Supper, Fra Angelico The Legend
of St Cosmas and Damian, among others.
3 Barbari Still Life, Mantegna Mucius Scaevola.
4 Filippo Lippi Madonna.
5 Vecchio, Lorenzo Lotto and Tintoretto.
6 Liss Cleopatra.
7 van Dyck Lamentation of Christ.
8 Rubens Landscape with Rainbow.
9 Rubens Susanna at the Bath.
10 Adriaen Brouwer.
11 Adam Elsheimer, Georg Flegel, Johann Rotten-
hammer.
12 Rubens, among others, The Fall of the Damned to
Hell and Medici Cycle.
14 Jan van Goyen, Pieter Claesz, Willem Kalf.
15 Pieter Lastmann.
16 Rembrandt Self-Portrait.
17 Adriaen van Ostade.
18 Jacob van Ruisdael, Meindert Hobbema.
19 Gerard Terborch, Nicolas Berchem.
20 Philips Wouverman, Pieter van Laer.
21–2 Jan Steen, Willem Kalf, Emanuel de Witte.
23 Giovanni Tiepolo, Rosalba Carriera.

The paintings displayed on the ground floor in the east
wing are mainly concerned with sacred themes, with the

exception of room IIa, which contains four late-Gothic portraits, as well as works by Dürer and other early-Renaissance artists. The west wing houses Dutch paintings from the 16th and 17th century.

Early German School (rooms I–III, cabinets 1–10): among others: Hans Pleydenwurf *Hof Altarpiece*, Lucas Cranach the Elder *Adam and Eve*, Michael Pacher *Altar of the Church Fathers*, Hans Burgkmaier the Elder *St John's Altar*, Hans Holbein the Elder *Kaisheim Altarpiece*, Stefan Lochner *Adoration of Christ*.

European Painting of the 16th and 17th century (rooms XII–XIII, cabinets 19–23): among others David Teniers the Younger, Giorgio Vasari, Lucas Cranach the Elder, Paul Bril *The Tower of Babel*, Hans von Aachen, Friedrich Sustris, Jan Brueghel the Elder *Troy Burning*, Pieter Brueghel the Elder *Fools Paradise*.

Directly across from the Alte Pinakothek is the ★★★ **Neue Pinakothek ⑳** . The foundation of the New Pinakothek was also laid by Ludwig I in 1846, because he wanted to have a building for works of art 'of his time'. The construction was carried out by the architect August von Voit, based on plans by Friedrich von Gärtner. In World War II the building was damaged so badly that it was decided to construct a new one. Designed by the Munich architect Alexander von Branca, this was finally opened in 1981.

The entrance hall displays works by Carl Rottmann on the right side (KR). Rooms A and B are reserved for changing exhibitions. The numbers in the following list are in accordance with the official numbering of the rooms.

The Neue Pinakothek foyer

48

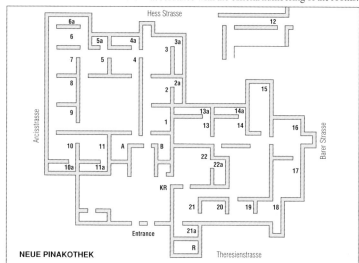

NEUE PINAKOTHEK

1–2A International art, about 1800 (David, Gains-borough, Canova, Goya, Turner, and others).

3–3A Early Romantic painters (Blechen, Friedrich, Dahl, Rottmann, Kobell, Kersting, Dillis).

4–4A Court art under Ludwig I (Stieler, Catel, von Hess, Thorvaldsen, Rebell, Wittmer, Bürkel).

5–5A German neoclassical painters in Rome (Koch, Reinhart, Hackert, Fries).

6A Small sculpture.

6 Georg Schäfer collection.

7 Nazarene (Overbeck, von Schadow, Olivier and Hess).

8–9 Biedermeier (Schwind, Quaglio, Adam, Wald-müller, Amerling, Alt).

10–10A French Late Romanticists and Realists (Gérecault, Corot, Courbet, Millet, Daumier, Delacroix).

11–11A German Late Romanticists and Realists (Menzel, Achenbach, Rayski, Spitzweg, Schleich, Volz).

12 Kaulbach's designs for the exterior embellish-ment of the original Neue Pinakothek.

13–13A Historical and social painting (Piloty and Vernet).

14–14A Painting from the *Gründerzeit*, the time of industrial expansion, about 1870 (Defregger, Munkascy, Markart, Schleich, Wenglein, Max, Keller, Lenbach).

15 Hans von Marées.

16 Böcklin, Feuerbach, Thoma.

17 Leibl and his circle (Schuch, Trübner).

18 French Impressionists (Manet, Monet, Degas, Pissaro and Renoir).

19 Cézanne, van Gogh, Gauguin, Rogin.

20 Social Realism (Liebermann, Slevogt, Uhde and Meunier).

21 German Impressionism (Corinth, Slevogt, Zügel).

21A Secessionists (Dill, Putz and others).

22–22A Symbolism and art nouveau (Klinger, Klimt, Hodler, Stuck, Khnopff, Toulouse-Lautrec, Vuil-lard, amongst others).

49

Van Gogh – Sunflowers

On the former Türkenkaserne, close to the Alte and Neue Pinakothek, an enormous new gallery, the **Pina-kothek der Moderne**, is due to be completed in the year 2,000. The complex will house, among other things, var-ious collections from the Haus der Kunst (*see page 53*), where there is no longer enough space, as well as the State Collection of the Graphic Arts and the Architecture Mu-seum of the Technical University.

In Theresienstrasse (entrance Barer Strasse opposite the Alte Pinakothek), the **Minerology Museum ⓶** (Miner-alogische Staatssammlung) contains interesting collec-tions from the world of minerals and crystals.

The Max II Monument on Maximilianstrasse

Route 8

19th-century Munich: Maximilianstrasse – Maximilianeum – Prinzregentenstrasse – Gallery of Modern Art (Haus der Kunst) – Bavarian National Museum – Prinzregententheater

New standards in urban planning were set by King Maximilian I, who designed the Maxvorstadt, and Ludwig I, who created his own architectural monument in the neoclassical Ludwigstrasse, but concepts for the extension of the city were commissioned by succeeding rulers as well. Thus King Maximilian II ordered the construction of Maximilianstrasse and Prince Regent Luitpold that of the long, west–east axis of Prinzregentenstrasse, already planned by Ludwig II, but not carried out during his reign.

A stylish concierge

In 1852 King Maximilian II (reigned 1848–64) had the construction of ★ **Maximilianstrasse** begun under the supervision of Friedrich Bürklein (1813–72). As the king put it 'a style representing the culture of these days' was to be discovered, which later came to be known in Munich as the Maximilian Style. It incorporates a synthesis of various architectural forms with a marked tendency for the vertical structuring typical of Gothic art. The street was planned as a connection between the city centre and the large open spaces of the Isar meadows. The king decided on a strictly structured street system at the beginning of the boulevard, which then opens and stretches in a broad and park-like manner down to the Isar. Modern traffic planning, however, rather spoiled the overall effect when the inner ring road was laid right across it.

The starting point for Maximilianstrasse is Max-Joseph-

Platz, with the loggia of the Post Office No 1 by Leo von Klenze and the National Theatre (*see page 28*). Opposite the opera house there is a row of commercial buildings, designed by Friedrich Bürklein in 1859–63. The **Hotel Vier Jahreszeiten**  was constructed in 1856–8 by Rudolph Wilhelm Gottgetreu, a pupil of the famous Berlin architect Karl Friedrich Schinkel, who had been offered a professor's chair at the erstwhile Technical Academy by Maximilian I.

On the other side of the street is the **Playhouse** ⓱ (Schauspielhaus). The building was erected by Max Littmann and Richard Riemerschmid in 1900–1 in art nouveau style. After its destruction in World War II, it was rebuilt according to the original plans, thus providing the city of Munich with one of the few pure art nouveau theatres in Germany.

Not far to the east of the Playhouse, Maximilianstrasse widens out like a forum. On the left is the building of the **Upper Bavarian Government** ⓲, one of the most outstanding examples of the Maximilian style. Strongly influenced by English Gothic, it was built in 1856–64 by Friedrich Bürklein. Above the ground floor, with its arcades, is a row of neo-Gothic arches of a markedly vertical character.

The seat of the Upper Bavarian Government

51

Opposite the government building is the newly refurbished **Völkerkundemuseum** ⓳. The Ethnological Museum, also greatly influenced by the English Gothic style, was erected by Eduard Riedel in 1858–65. The museum, for which the first exhibits were collected by Ludwig I,

MVSEVM FVR VOLKERKVNDE

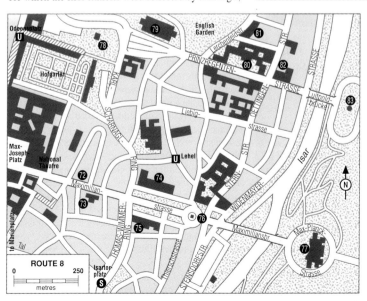

possesses a fine collection of non-European cultural items from countries all over the world. In particular, ★ works of art and objects of everyday use from Africa, Central and South Asia, East Asia, Oceania and Latin America are represented. Special exhibitions enable the house to make more of its comprehensive collection accessible to the public from time to time, and the museum also hosts numerous temporary exhibitions.

In the park between the two last-mentioned buildings are bronze statues, created in 1858–63: on the north side are the Bavarian general Count Deroy (1743–1812) and the father of the English Garden, Count Rumford (Benjamin Thompson, 1753–1814); on the south side are statues of the philosopher Friedrich Wilhelm Schelling (1755–1854) and the physicist and astronomer Joseph Fraunhofer (1787–1826).

Towards the Isar, in the centre of Maximilianstrasse, is the **Max II Monument** 🕖. Kaspar von Zumbusch created this monument in 1875 to the memory of King Maximilian II, who promoted art, science and social progress. The four great bronze figures are allegorical representations of the four virtues of a ruler.

To the northwest, at St-Anna-Platz, is the ★ **Monastery Church of St Anne**, built by Johann Michael Fischer in 1727–33, the first rococo church in Old Bavaria. The Isar is spanned by the Maximiliansbrücke. On a high pedestal stands the statue of Pallas Athene, symbolising Munich as a city of art.

Back now in Maximilianstrasse, looking across to the other bank of the Isar the view is dominated by the Maximilianeum 🕖. The foundation stone to this monumental building was laid in 1857 by Friedrich Bürklein, who did not live to see the project through to its completion in 1874. Through Gottfried Semper's influence, the pointed-arch architecture of Bürklein was converted to neo-Romanesque forms.

In 1876 the building became the home of the Maximilianeum Foundation for Gifted Bavarian Students, which offered the most gifted pupils in the country free and adequate accomodation, thus enabling them to complete their studies and training for high state posts without any financial worries. Since 1949 the Maximilianeum has been the home of the Bavarian Landtag, or parliament, and its Senate, the advisory second chamber. For these institutions extensions were built to the east in 1957–60. The balustrade in front of the Maximilianeum is open to visitors and offers a marvellous view of the city and the parks along the banks of the river Isar.

The last great urban extension in the 19th century was **Prinzregentenstrasse**, the construction of which was

Detail of the Maximilianeum

The Prinz Carl Palais

begun in 1890. At the beginning of the street stands a building from an earlier era, the **Prinz Carl Palais** built by Carl von Fischer in early-neoclassical style for the minister Abbé von Salabert. From 1825 it served as residence for Prince Carl (died 1875). In 1826 Jean-Baptist Métivier extended the western part of the building. In 1937 Gablonsky partly rebuilt the edifice in an elegant fashion. The Prince Carl Palace is the most beautiful early-neoclassical building in Munich. Today the palace serves as a seat of representation for the Bavarian minister-president. The removal of an adjacent traffic roundabout has restored at least some of the original dignity to the palace's setting; the busy inner ring road tunnels right underneath the building.

On the opposite, left-hand side of Prinzregentenstrasse, stands the ★ **Haus der Kunst** ⑦. The House of Art was erected in 1933–7 as a substitute for the Glass Palace in the Old Botanical Garden, which burnt down in 1931. It was built as an exhibition hall by Paul Ludwig Troost in the monumental style typical of the Third Reich.

While changing exhibitions are held in the east and middle sections of the 160-m (525-ft) long neoclassical building, the west wing has since 1946 housed the ★★ **Gallery of Modern Art** (Staatsgalerie Moderner Kunst). The emphasis here is placed on the collection of contemporary works of art. The rooms are arranged as follows:

Ground floor

1. Changing exhibitions.
2. Fauves and Expressionists (eg Matisse, Corinth, Kokoschka).
3. Ernst Ludwig Kirchner – Wilhelm Lehmbruck.
4. *Brücke* and *Blauer Reiter*.
5. Cubism (eg Braque, Picasso).
6. Orphism and Cubo-Futurism (eg Chagall, Delaunay, Boccioni).
7. Bauhaus and Constructivism.
8. Paul Klee.

9, 11–12 Surrealist Collection (eg Dalí).

10. Günter Franke Foundation – Max Beckmann.

13–14 Representative tendencies since the 1920s (eg Carrà, Morandi).

15. Pablo Picasso, Henri Laurens.
16. Sofie and Emanuel Fohn Donation (eg Marc, Macke, Dix).
17. Hans Hartung Foundation.
18. Abstract Art of the 1940s, 1950s and 1960s (eg Baumeister, Nay, Jorn).
19. Antoni Tàpies, Francis Bacon, Henry Moore.
20. Marino Marini Foundation.
21. Robert Motherwell Foundation.

The sign to the gallery

Bavarian National Museum: exhibit from the Hall of Armour

Further east on the left-hand side of Prinzregentenstrasse (beyond Lerchenfeldstrasse) is the ★★ **Bavarian National Museum** ⚈. This building was erected by Gabriel von Seidl in 1894–1900. Even the museum's exterior mirrors the various artistic periods represented in it: the east wing the Romanesque period, the west wing the Renaissance, the middle section with its tower the early baroque and the building to the west the rococo. In front of the east wing is an equestrian statue of Prince Regent Luitpold, designed by Adolf von Hildebrand in 1901–3.

The collections in the museum date back to an exhibition arranged by Maximilian II in the Maxburg in 1855. They are divided into two main sections: the art historical collection and the folklore collection. Some of the rooms are temporarily closed due to renovation work. A notice in the foyer provides information about the current status of the various rooms.

Ground floor

1–21 Middle Ages. The following rooms deserve special attention: 1 (Wessobrunn room), 2 (Room of the Virgin with the rose bush), 4 (Bam-

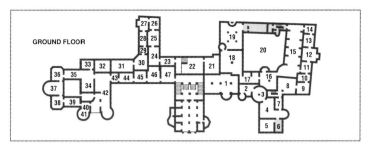

GROUND FLOOR

berg room), 8 (Multscher room), 11 (Füssen room), 13 (Room of Flemish tapestry), 15 (Room of churches), 16 (Riemenschneider room), 17 (late-Gothic, c 1500), 18 (Hall of Armour), 21 (Leineberger room).

22–30 Renaissance. The following are particularly important: 22 (German Renaissance), 23 (Italian Renaissance), 25 (Paulaner chapel), 26 (late-Italian Renaissance), 28 (Laiunger room), 29 (late-German Renaissance), 30 (Wilhelm V room). This department also contains the models of cities that used to be on the first floor.

31–43 Baroque and rococo. The following are worthy of note: 31 (Maximilian room), 32 (Henriette Adelaide room), 33 and 34 (Max-Emanuel rooms), 38 (Religious crafts of the 18th century), 42 and 43 (Ignaz Günther rooms).

44–46 Classicism: The King's rooms.

First floor

51 Glass painting.
52 Miniatures.
53–54 Baroque sketches.
57 Inlaid wood.
58–59 Watches.
69 Art nouveau objects.
71–73 Special exhibition.

Exterior of the Bavarian National Museum

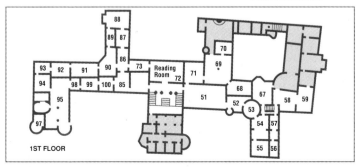

1ST FLOOR

Stained glass exhibit

About 100m to the west of the main building is the **New Collection** (Die Neue Sammlung), which was opened in 1981 as an independent Museum of Applied Art. Behind the Bavarian National Museum in Lerchenfeldstrasse is the modern building of the ★ **Prehistoric Collection** ❸❶ (Prähistorische Staatssammlung), which provides information about the cultural periods in Bavaria from Paleolithic times up to the early Middle Ages. Changing exhibitions with prehistoric and culturally important historic items are held here as well. The permanent exhibition is divided into the following cultural periods: Stone Age (room 1), Bronze Age (up to the 13th century BC, room 2), Urn Field Age (up to the 8th century BC, room 3), Hallstatt Age (up to 500BC, room 4), Latène Age (up to 15BC, room 5), Manching (settlement of the late Latène Age, room 6), Roman Era I–III (rooms 7–9), Alemanni,

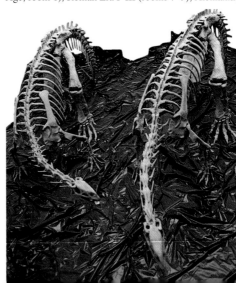

Bavarians, Franconians (5th to 7th century, room 10), Merovingian and Carolingian eras (room 11), early Middle Ages up to the founding of Munich (room 12).

Following Prinzregentenstrasse towards the Isar, you come to the building of the ★ **Schackgalerie** . Commissioned by Emperor Wilhelm II, it was erected by Max Littmann in 1907–9 in conjunction with the Prussian Embassy Building (until recently the Bavarian State Chancellery). During the second half of the 19th century Adolf Friedrich von Schack (1815–94), a former Prussian state official, collected numerous masterpieces by contemporary artists, which led Wilhelm II to bestow upon him the title of count. In his will Schack left his collection to the emperor, who insisted that the paintings should remain in the city of Munich.

Schack's private collection, which was incorporated in the Bavarian State Picture Collection in 1939, includes paintings dating from the early-Romantic period through to works by Moritz von Schwind, Carl Spitzweg, Arnold Böcklin, and many others

Crossing Prinzregentenbrücke (bridge), you encounter a work of art dominating the park along the other side of the Isar, the **Friedensengel** . The Angel of Peace Monument, donated by the city of Munich in 1896 in remembrance of the preliminary Peace of Versailles and in gratitude to the Bavarian army, consists of a terrace in Florentine style and a 23-m (75-ft) high column topped by an angel meant to resemble the goddess of victory (Nike) in Olympia.

The Angel of Peace

57

Farther east in Prinzregentenstrasse (No 60), in the well-to-do district of Bogenhausen, is the elegant **Stuckvilla**. It was built in 1897–8 according to plans of the owner, the Munich 'prince of painters' Franz von Stuck (1863–1923). The interior decoration of the house is a prime example of art nouveau (original frescoes, paintings, graphic drawings and documentation from about 1900). The building, which is today the property of the city, also houses various galleries for special exhibitions. The bronze figure in front of the neoclassical main entrance, a spear-throwing Amazon, is based on a design by Stuck.

Also in keeping with the elegance of the area is the delicatessen **Feinkost Käfer**, on the left-hand side of the Prinzregentenstrasse going east. Further east at Prinzregentenplatz is the **Prinzregententheater**. The Prince Regent's Theatre was constructed in 1899–1901 according to the draft plans of Gottfried Semper for the Wagner festival theatre, planned by Ludwig II. After years of painstaking restorations, which saw the building returned to its former glory, the theatre was re-opened with great ceremony at the beginning of 1988.

Route 9

The West: Theresienwiese – Messegelände – Westpark

From the main railway station (U- and S-Bahn) follow Bayerstrasse in a westerly direction and turn left into Hermann-Lingg-Strasse.

Before arriving at the Bavariaring you will see the **Parish Church of St Paul** 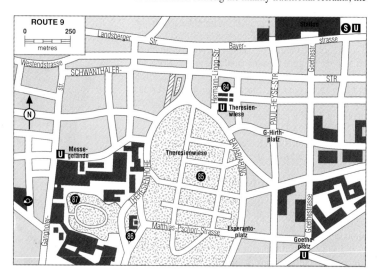 on the left. The basilica with its three aisles was built in neo-Gothic style between 1892 and 1906 by Georg Hauberrisser.

The Bavariaring forms the eastern boundary of the **Theresienwiese** or meadow. Its history dates back to a horse race held on 17 October 1810, in honour of the wedding of Crown Prince Ludwig and Therese von Sachsen-Hildburghausen. The memory of the folk festival held to mark the occasion is still kept alive by the world-famous Oktoberfest. For a long time, the Oktoberfest, or Weis'n as it is affectionately called by Bavarians, remained a local agricultural fair attended exclusively by the people of Munich and farmers from the outlying countryside. But by the latter part of the 20th century, the original meadow had been turned to concrete and the small booths selling food and beer had been replaced by enormous temporary beer halls, each accommodating over 6,000 people; the fair had developed into a gigantic festival, where visitors no longer arrived in their thousands, but in their millions – from all over the world.

Each 'tent' belongs to one of Munich's six major breweries, and each has its own brass band occupying a podium in the middle. Among the mainly traditional refrains, the

Oktoberfest fun

call of *eins, zwei, drei G' Suffa* (one, two, three, drink)
exhorts the revellers to empty their glasses and order more
beer from the well-built Bavarian waitresses. But the beer
tents do not provide the only action at the Oktoberfest: one
side of the Theresienwiese is taken up by all the usual
fairground paraphernalia, interspersed by stalls selling
everything from candyfloss to curried sausage.

The opening parade

59

But for most of the year, the Theresienwiese is noth-
ing more than a large area of waste ground. Its west flank
is dominated by the **Bavaria** and the **Hall of Fame** . Including its base, the monument of the Bavaria is about 30m
(98ft) high. The bronze statue itself measures 15.8m (52
ft). The design for the bronze figure was by Schwanthaler,
the figure was cast by Ferdinand von Miller in 1844–50.
The Bavaria can be climbed from the inside by a spiral
staircase (130 steps). Five small openings in the head offer a splendid view of the city (daily except Monday
10am–noon and 2–5.30pm).

The Bavaria

Ludwig I commissioned not only the Bavaria, but also
the Ruhmeshalle or Hall of Fame. Between 1843 and 1853
Leo von Klenze built this open, colonnaded hall in the style
of a Doric temple to honour deserving Bavarians.

Behind the Bavaria on the Theresienhöhe or heights
extends the **Messegelände** . Around 30 international
fairs and exhibitions as well as 60 other events take place
at this exhibition centre each year, encompassing all lines
of business from fashion to tourism to machinery.

The newly created **Westpark**, further southwest in
Untersendling and crossed by the Garmischer Strasse
(Westpark U-Bahn 3 and U-Bahn 6), was the scene of the
1983 International Horticultural Exhibition. The park is
now a particularly interesting site with beautiful fountains,
Chinese, Thai and Japanese temples, a restaurant in the
Rosengarten, a waterside café and also two beer gardens.

The Olympic Park

The Outskirts

★★ *Olympic Park*

The sport and recreation area of the Olympic Park, comprising 2.8sq km (1.1sq miles), was laid out on the occasion of the 20th Summer Olympics in 1972. On the site of Oberwiesenfeld, a former royal Bavarian parade ground, the construction of buildings and sports facilities was begun in 1968. The Schuttberg (a hill built out of the rubble of houses destroyed in Munich during World War II) was also included. It is the present 52-m (171-ft) high Olympiaberg, from which, on a clear day, there is a magnificent view of the city and the Alps beyond. The park can be reached easily from the city centre with the U-Bahn 2, U-Bahn 3 or tram Nos 20, 25, 27.

The **Fernsehturm** (Television Tower), the symbol of the Summer Olympics, and also called Olympiaturm or tower, is almost 290m (950ft) high and dominates the whole complex. Above the postal installations there are a revolving restaurant and observation terraces (daily 9am–12pm, lift fee DM5, children from 6–17 DM2.50) from where you get a splendid view of the city; on days with *Föhn* (*see page 6*) even the distant Alps seem to be close enough to touch.

The impressive ★★ **Olympic Stadium**, like the Olympia Hall and Olympia Swimming Pool, was designed by the architects Behnisch and Partners (1968–72) and can accommodate about 78,000 people. The Olympia Hall can hold up to 14,000 people. It is the venue for athletic and cultural events as well as exhibitions and congresses.

With its costs of construction at 168 million marks the 74,800-sq m (89,460-sq yd) ★★ **Tent Roof** was the most expensive one in the world. The construction consists of a tubular network, covered with transparent tiles of acrylic plastic, hung from 12 masts up to 81m (265 ft) high.

The **Ice Skating Stadium** (7,200 spectators) at the entrance to the Olympic Park was built by R Schütze, and the Ice Skating Rink just next to it was conceived by the architect Ackermann. The Olympia Radstadion or Cycle Stadium (5,100 spectators) at the end of the park was erected by the architects Beier and Partners. To the south of the sports facilities is the Olympiasee, an artificial lake. The Theatron, a floating stage, is also located here. It is used for open-air events, especially pop concerts.

Southwest of the Olympiaberg, amidst a once well-cultivated garden, there stands a Russian Orthodox chapel. It was built after World War II by a Russian recluse, known as *Väterchen Timofej* (Father Timothy).

The Olympic Village lies to the north of the Mittlerer Ring. The high-rise buildings, designed by the architectural association Heinle, Wischer and Partners, formed the village for male participants; the low buildings, created by Eckert and Wirsing, were the village for female participants. While the high-rise apartments of the men's village have been sold as owner-occupied flats, after the Olympic Games the women's village was given over to student accommodation.

Situated to the north of the ring road and accessible via a foot bridge, the administrative tower of the **Bavarian**

The Olympic Village

61

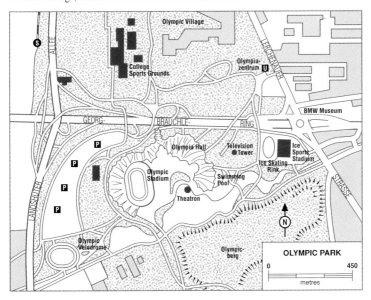

Motor Works (BMW) rises almost 100m (328 ft) high. Next to it there is the bowl-shaped concrete building of the **BMW Museum**, which is devoted to technical developments, social history and future prospects; there is a collection of classic motor-cars, motor-cycles and aircraft engines as well as tools of the car manufacturing industry, including robots.

⋆⋆ *Tierpark Hellabrunn*

At the zoo

Hellabrunn Zoo was laid out in 1911 according to plans by Emanuel Seidl, under the patronage of Prince Regent Luitpold. Its name dates back to a mansion once located here. In 1928 Heinz Heck, zoologist and director of the zoo, gave the complex its present form. The grounds cover 70ha (173 acres). It can be reached by the U-Bahn 3 to Thalkirchen, the No 57 bus from Sendlinger Tor, or the No 52 bus from Marienplatz (summer 8am–6pm, winter 9am–5pm; animal houses close about half an hour earlier; admission charge).

Hellabrunn Zoo was the first 'geographical zoo' in the world. That means the animals here are arranged according to their continent of origin (Europe, America, Australia, Africa, Asia and the polar regions). An attempt has been made to reproduce specific climatic regions, thus pro-

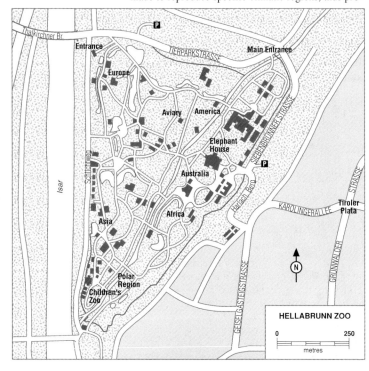

viding the animals with the most home-like conditions. The method has had considerable success. The Munich zoo is one of high birthrates. The breeding of endangered species as well as of animals that no longer exist in the wild, such as the tarpan, a European wild horse, have been very successful. Animals of special interest in the zoo are the bison, white-tailed gnu, ibex, onager, wild banteng, Père David's deer and armoured rhinoceros. Especially popular is the anthropoid ape section, which breeds more chimpanzees than any other zoo in Europe.

The only enclosure housing animals from all continents is the large **aviary** for about 200 birds, which was opened in 1980. The latest addition to the zoo is the **jungle enclosure**, covered with a perspex tent, where lions and jaguars, apes and exotic birds can all be viewed at close quarters. Other superlative attractions include the penguin and polar bear enclosure, the largest in Europe, and an aquarium with about 40 basins for aquatic animals from all parts of the world. A special attraction for the young is the **children's zoo**, with ponies and dwarf species of donkeys, monkeys and goats – all to be stroked.

63

★★ *Nymphenburg Palace and Park*

Nymphenburg Palace is about 8km (5 miles) from the centre of Munich and can be reached on the No 12 tram and the No 41 bus. (Palace and Amalienburg, 1 April to 30 September 9am–12.30pm, 1.30–5pm; winter 10am–12.30pm and 1.30–4pm. Pagodenburg and Magdalenen-klause summer only 10am–12.30pm, 1.30–5pm. Marstall-museum summer daily 9am–noon, 1–5pm; winter 10am–noon and 1–4pm, except Monday. All buildings except the Amalienburg closed Monday. Admission charge for all buildings on a collective ticket.)

★★ **Nymphenburg Palace** has a long and colourful history. Out of gratitude for the birth of his heir Max Emanuel, Elector Ferdinand Maria presented his wife, Henriette Adelaide of Savoy, with the *Schwaige* or dairy farm out to the west of the city. At first the centre building with its double flight of outdoor steps was erected, to serve as the summer residence of the Wittelsbachs. Work was begun by the Italian, Agostino Barelli, in 1664; it was continued by Enrico Zuccalli from 1673 and ultimately completed in 1675.

Nymphenburg Palace

In 1702–4, during the reign of Elector Maximilian II Emanuel, Antonio Viscardi added the four cubic pavilions, connecting them with the central building by arcades according to plans by Zuccalli; the two eastern pavilions were finished in 1716 by Joseph Effner.

In 1719 the palace was extended again. To the south the Marstall (stables) was built and in 1723–4 to the north – as a counterpart – the four-winged complex of the Orang-

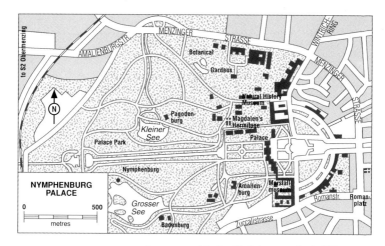

The Steinerner Saal ceiling

Lola Montez

erie was erected, both with their connecting buildings. The garden pavilions also date from these years.

François de Cuvilliés was commissioned by Elector Karl Albrecht to design the great crescent in front of the palace (1729–58), with the houses of the court officials. In the middle building in the northeast of the semi-circle the **Nymphenburg Porcelain Manufactory**, founded in 1747, was housed. House No 1, in the southern section of the crescent, contains the Erwin von Kreibig Museum, with works by this Munich painter and graphic designer (1904–61) and special exhibitions featuring the work of young Munich artists.

Maximilian III Joseph rebuilt the palace on the inside. Thus in 1755–7 he gave the great hall, the Steinerner Saal, its present splendour through the work of Cuvilliés and Johann Baptist Zimmermann.

The **Steinerner Saal**, the two-storey festive hall in the centre building, goes back to plans by Enrico Zuccalli and Joseph Effner. The ceiling frescoes are by Johann Baptist Zimmermann. The former small refectory in the south pavilion became Ludwig I's famous **Gallery of Beauties** or Schönheitsgalerie, painted by Josef Stieler between 1827 and 1850. It includes a painting of the famous Irish dancer Lola Montez, whose affair with Ludwig I was one of the reasons for his abdication in 1848.

★★**Nymphenburg Palace Park** (daily 6am–dusk) grew together with the palace. What was originally an Italian garden (1671) was later turned into a French, baroque-style park and finally transformed into a great English park of 221ha (546 acres) by Friedrich Ludwig Schell in 1803–5.

At the back of the palace the grand parterre, all that remains of the original French garden, stretches away to the west. The eye travels from the straight middle axis (decorated on both sides with stone sculptures of Greek gods) to the main canal with a cascade at the end, which was built by Dominique Girard in 1731.

There are several pavilions scattered over the park. Left of the grand parterre is the ★★★ **Amalienburg**, a hunting lodge built by Elector Karl Albrecht for his wife Maria Amalia. This little pleasure palace, erected in 1734–9, is a masterpiece of Cuvilliés' rococo. Around the centre of the building, the round Hall of Mirrors, several rooms are clustered, such as the Blue Cabinet (the bedroom of the Electress), the Hunting Room (with rifle cabinets above the kennels of the pack of hounds) and the Pheasant Room.

Amalienburg

Deeper within the park and also on the left-hand side of the canal, you come to the ★ **Badenburg**, built by Joseph Effner from 1718–21 in French style. The rich stucco ornamentation was the work of Charles Claude Debut. The lodge took its name from the large bathing room complete with heated pool, which Elector Maximilian II Emanuel had constructed here.

On the other side of the Badenburg Lake is the Temple of Apollo. At the cascade, cross the middle axis and turn northeast, thus reaching the ★ **Pagodenburg**, erected in octagonal form by Joseph Effner in 1716–19. François Cuvilliés renewed the facade and the interior decorations in 1767. The little palace took its name from the pagodas painted in the Chinese style by Johann Anton Gumpp.

In the Pagodenburg   **65**

Further east, towards Nymphenburg Palace, you come to the **Magdalenenklause** or Magdalen's Hermitage, which Maximilian II Emanuel had built as a hermitage for himself. Effner erected this artificial ruin with a grotto chapel in 1725. The stucco statue of Mary Magdalen was the work of Giuseppe Volponi (1726). The ceiling painting was created by Nikolaus Gottfried Stuber.

Leave the park and turn right to arrive at the ★ **Marstallmuseum**, located in the Wittelsbachs' former coachhouse in the south wing of Nymphenburg Palace. State coaches, sledges, harnesses and riding equipment are on display. The first floor of the museum houses a large special collection of Nymphenburg Porcelain (Bäuml Collection).

In the north wing of the palace you will find the **Museum Mensch und Natur** (Natural History Museum), which focuses on the history of the earth, the diversity of life, the biology of man and his relationship to the environment (daily except Monday 9am–5pm).

Immediately adjacent to Nymphenburg Park are the ★ **Botanical Gardens**, which can easily be reached on the No 12 tram. They were laid out in 1909–14 and contain, for example, special sections devoted to ★ alpine flora and rhododendrons. (Grounds, summer 9am–6pm, winter 9am–4.30pm; greenhouses, summer 9–11.45am and 1–5.30pmr, winter 9–11.45am and 1–4pm; admission fee.)

Blutenburg Castle

Additional Sights

The suburbs of Munich contain a wealth of sights, including churches and country houses, all of which are well worth a visit.

A detail of the Castle Chapel

Situated to the west of the city, near the beginning of the motorway to Stuttgart, **Blutenburg Castle** (Obermenzing; No 73 bus from Nymphenburg) is a late-Gothic jewel. Even before the time of Duke Sigismund there was a hunting lodge here, built by Duke Albrecht III in 1439. At that time the building was still surrounded by the Würm river, and it served as a love nest for the duke and Agnes Bernauer (who was accused of being a witch and died in the Danube at Straubing). During the Thirty Years War it was partially burnt down, and was rebuilt in 1681. Today the Blutenburg houses the International Youth Library. The Blutenburg concerts are well known.

The adjacent ★ **Blutenburg Castle Chapel** is the finest feature of the castle complex. Erected in 1488 on the orders of Duke Sigismund, it is a splendid masterpiece of the late-Gothic style. The stained-glass windows and the vaulting are beautiful enough, but truly unforgettable is the main ★ **altarpiece** by Jan Polack, depicting the *Throne of Mercy* with the body of Christ resting in the lap of God, flanked on the two wings by the *Coronation of the Virgin* and the *Baptism of Christ*. Exquisite, too, are the limewood figures of Christ, the 12 apostles, and the famous ★ **Blutenburg Madonna**.

Like Blutenburg Castle Chapel, the late-Gothic **Church of St Martin** in Untermenzing (No 76 bus from Blutenburg) was donated by Duke Sigismund. In this church, built by Ulrich Randeck in 1499, the six Gothic stained-glass windows (1499) and the paintings of the high altar (beginning of the 17th century) are of particular interest.

The **Parish Church St Wolfgang** in Pipping (Pippinger Strasse 49a; 10 minutes by foot from Blutenburg Castle) was also built under Duke Sigismund, 10 years before he commissioned the construction of Blutenburg Castle Chapel. This late-Gothic treasure, erected in 1478, has survived almost unaltered and undamaged. Jan Polack created the paintings in the chancel and on the walls (1479). The stained-glass windows date from the year 1478. The tree-carved altars, dating from the period when the church was built, are worth mentioning, although it is not known who executed them.

The **Parish Church of St Ulrich** in Laim (Agnes-Bernauer-Strasse 104; Nos 19 and 29 trams, S-Bahn 1 and 2) dates back to a chapel of the 11th century, belonging to a large estate. The choir and the tower are 15th-century late-Gothic.

The baroque **Church of St George** in Bogenhausen (Neuberghauser Strasse; Nos 18 and 20 trams) was built by Johann Michael Fischer in 1759. It is situated in the middle of an idyllic churchyard, where well-known Munich citizens, including Liesl Karlstadt, Erich Kästner and Hans Knappertsbusch, were laid to rest. Originally a Romanesque construction had stood here. The frescoes, completed in 1770, were the work of Philipp Helterhof, the high altar with St George on horseback is by Johann Baptist Straub, and the pulpit and the righ-hand altar are by Ignaz Günther.

67

The grave of Erich Kästner

The **★ Church of St Michael** in Berg am Laim (U-Bahn 2) is one of the most delightful of all Bavarian rococo churches. The Prince Bishop Clemens August of Cologne, the nephew of Elector Maximilian II Emanuel, had it created for the Knights' Order of St Michael; it was built by Johann Michael Fischer between 1735 and 1758. The stucco and frescoes were created by Johann Baptist Zimmermann in 1743, the side altars (1743–59) as well as the high altar (1767) were constructed by Johann Baptist Strauss, while the pulpit was the work of Benedikt Hassler (1745).

The tower of St Michael's

St Stephen's, also in Berg am Laim (Baumkirchner Strasse 45; S-Bahn 4 and 6), is the first church mentioned in documents about Munich. Even before the city was founded it was part of the imperial possessions, until 1052, when it passed over to the bishop of Freising. The late-Gothic church building was erected by Lukas Rottaler in about 1510; the interior was recreated in baroque style in 1713.

As early as the 14th century the **Parish Church of St Mary** in Ramersdorf (Aribonenstrasse 9; U-Bahn 2 to Karl-Preis-Platz, then bus 95) was one of the favourite

places of pilgrimage in Old Bavaria. The church, dating back to the 11th century, was replaced by a new construction in Gothic style at the beginning of the 15th century and had baroque elements added in 1675. Inside, the ★ *Virgin* on the high altar, the ★ *Crucifixion* by Erasmus Grasser (1510) and the paintings by Jan Polack (1483) on the winged altar-piece, as well as a votive painting of the 42 hostages taken by Gustavus Adolphus of Sweden (Matthias Kager, 1635) are all worth closer inspection.

Probably founded in the 14th century, the **Parish Church of St Mary** in Thalkirchen (Frauenbergplatz 1; U-Bahn 3; 31 and 57 buses) acquired its baroque form in 1692. The ★ high altar with its late-Gothic *Virgin and Child* by Gregor Erhart (1482) was given its present form by Ignaz Günther.

The interior of St Mary's

Dating from the beginning of the 15th century, the single-aisled late-Gothic **Parish Church of the Holy Cross** in Forstenried (Forstenrieder Allee 180a; U-Bahn 3) was redone in baroque style on the inside by Gasparo Zuccalli. The high altar is decorated with a late-Romanesque ★ wooden crucifix, which was probably carved about 1200 in the monastery at Seeon. It is the only masterpiece of that era still located in a Munich church.

The **Church of St John Baptist** in Johanneskirchen (Gleissenbachstrasse 2; S-Bahn 3) forms the focal point of the village and dates back to the 13th century. The frescoes on the north wall are from the 14th century, the portal dates from 1520. In 1688 a new ceiling vault with stucco was installed. The high altar with statues by Ignaz Günther is worth seeing.

The **Church of St Laurence** in Oberföhring (Muspillistrasse 14; 88 and 188 buses) was built by Wolfgang Zwerger in 1680. The high altar is from the same year. It contains some beautiful stucco work.

The palace at **Fürstenried** (Forst-Kasten-Allee; 34 bus from Pasing) is a miniature version of Nymphenburg. Commissioned by Elector Maximilian II Emanuel, Joseph Effner built this former hunting lodge in 1715–17. It later served as a place of residence for the Electress Anna Maria from 1778 to 1796. From the symmetrically laid out complex an avenue of lime trees points straight towards the Frauenkirche (8km/5 miles away). Sadly, the view along the avenue is today interrupted by the Munich-Garmisch motorway.

The **Asam Estate of St Mary Anchorite** or **Maria Ensiedel** (Benediktbeurer Strasse 19; Nos 31 and 57 buses and a 10-minute walk; No 66 bus from Harras) was acquired by the rococo sculptor and painter Cosmas Damian Asam in 1724. He converted and extended the building, painting the facade in a style then widespread in Munich – with allegories, saints and architectural perspectives.

Excursions

A number of places of great cultural and historical interest can be easily reached from Munich by S-Bahn.

Along the Isar Valley

As early as Celtic and Roman times fortifications were built above the banks of the Isar. In 1293 the Wittelsbachs built a castle in **Grünwald** (No 25 tram, S-Bahn 7 to Höllriegelskreuth), where Emperor Ludwig the Bavarian (1287–1347) spent his youth and which was given its present form in the 15th century. Nowadays the castle contains an interesting museum (*see page 80*).

The famous Benedictine abbey **Kloster Schäftlarn** (S-Bahn 7 to Hohenschäftlarn) was founded as early as 782. The present complex was erected in 1702–57, the monastery buildings according to plans by Giovanni Antonio Viscardi, the ★ monastery church at first according to drafts by François de Cuvilliés, later to those of Johann Baptist Gunezrhainer. The stucco work was by Johann Baptist Zimmermann. Johann Baptist Straub created the altars and the pulpit. Concerts are regularly held in the monastery, whose appeal is further enhanced in the summertime by the adjacent beer garden.

69

Lake Starnberg

The chief town of the 20-km (12-mile) long, up to 5-km (3-mile) wide lake (regular boat service in summer) is **Starnberg** (pop. 17,500; S-Bahn 6), located at the north end. The town grew up around a medieval castle. A boldly curved bridge leads from the castle (1541, now seat of a revenue office) to the old ★ **Parish Church of St Joseph** (1770), a charming late-rococo building. The high altar of this church is by Ignaz Günther.

Bernried, a small town on the western shore of the lake, has become known for its former Augustinian canons' monastery, dating back to a double monastery founded in 1121. St Martin's Church has a carved wooden winged altar dating from 1484.

The eastern shore of the lake is more remote and inaccessible than the western shore. The village of **Berg** has a castle built in 1640 and renovated several times, which now serves as a residence for Prince Albrecht von Bayern (an hereditary title). The late-Romanesque church contains the wooden relief *Death of the Virgin* from the 15th century. On the shore of the lake is the neo-Romanesque Memorial Chapel (1900) for Ludwig II, the fairy-tale king who was found drowned here in the lake together with his physician on 13 June 1886, at a place now marked by a cross. The anniversary of his death is still marked by an annual pilgrimage in his honour.

Lake Starnberg

Andechs Abbey

Ammersee

Herrsching (pop. 8,600; S-Bahn 5) is the main town in the Ammersee region, to the west of Lake Starnberg. The lake (regular boat service in summer) is 16km (10 miles) long and up to 6km (4 miles) wide. On the ridge of a moraine, above Herrsching, is the Heiliger Berg (Holy Mountain) with the famous ★ **Benedictine Abbey of Andechs**. It can be reached either by road or along the picturesque footpath that winds its way up through the woods from Herrsching – the walk takes about an hour. The monastery and pilgrimage church of the Annunciation stands on a site formerly occupied by a castle belonging to the Counts of Andechs. The church was begun in 1438 and given its baroque form in 1751. The baroque interior decorations are by Johann Baptist Zimmermann. Very impressive is the ★ **high altar** with the miraculous image of the **Virgin enthroned**. Andechs is also world famous for its monastic brewery and the adjacent **beer garden** is a magnet for tourists during the summer months. The beer is served by the monks themselves.

The Virgin enthroned

On the southwest shore of the lake (bus and boat connections) lies **Diessen** (pop. 7,500). It is dominated by ★★ **St Mary's Church**, which once belonged to the Augustinians and was erected by Johann Michael Fischer in 1732–9. The ceiling frescoes were created by Johann Georg Bergmüller, and the stucco was the work of Johann Michael Feichtmayr. François de Cuvilliés designed the ★ high altar, which was then completed by Joachim Dietrich. Also worthy of note are the pulpit by Johann Baptist Straub and the angel figure by the famous sculptor Ignaz Günther (10.30am–noon and 2pm–6pm; guided tours at 11am and 2pm).

Fürstenfeldbruck

About 23km (14 miles) west of Munich on the Amper river is the town of Fürstenfeldbruck (pop. 32,000; S-Bahn 4). The ★ **Church of the Assumption** was begun in 1701 according to plans by Giovanni Antonio Viscardi and completed in 1718–36 by Johann Georg Ettenhofer. The frescoes were the work of the two Asam brothers. The stucco was by Egid Quirin Asam, who also designed the high altar. The two statues of Ludwig the Stern and Ludwig the Bavarian were created by Roman Anton Boos.

The palace at Dachau

The Dachau region

Northwest of Munich (8km/11 miles), on the steep bank of the Amper river, is the town of **Dachau** (pop. 35,000; S-Bahn 2). In the 11th century a subsidiary line of the Wittelsbachs, Scheyern-Dachau, built a castle here, around which the place developed. In 1391 it became a market, in 1934 a town. The present **palace** is all that remains of a four-winged Renaissance building, erected by the dukes Wilhelm IV and Albrecht V according to plans by Heinrich Schöttl. The renovation work in 1715 was supervised by Dachau-born Joseph Effner. At the beginning of the 19th century the complex fell into ruin, with the exception of the southwest tract. The Parish Church of St James was built in its present form in 1624–5 according to a plan by Hans Krumper.

On the eastern edge of the town there is a place of remembrance for one of the Third Reich's most barbarous concentration camps. The complex, laid out as a memorial in 1965, has a museum with about 500 objects documenting the horrors of Dachau and other Nazi concentration camps.

A place of remembrance

At nearby **Markt Indersdorf** (pop. 6,700; S-Bahn 2), the foundation of the monastery formerly belonging to the Augustinian canons dates back to a donation by Duke Otto VI of the Palatinate (about 1120). The late-Romanesque monastery church was redone in baroque style in the middle of the 18th century. Worth seeing are the ★ **high altar**, decorated with figures by Andreas Faistenberger and a wall fresco by Johann Andreas Wolf.

The former ★ **Benedictine monastery church** of St Peter in **Petersberg** (connection with S-Bahn 2) was built in 1104–7, and is one of the most beautiful Romanesque churches still existing in Bavaria. The frescoes of the choir deserve special attention.

At **Altomünster** (connection with S-Bahn 2), the Benedictine double monastery of St Alto was founded as long ago as 750. Since 1485 it has served the Order of St Bridget (it is the only St Bridget convent in Germany). The ★ **monastery church** was begun by Johann Michael

Fischer in 1763. Worth seeing is the interior decoration, which was partly completed by Johann Baptist Straub and Jakob Rauch.

Schleissheim

About 15km (9 miles) north of Munich, easily accessible via the Nuremberg Autobahn or S-Bahn 1, is the suburb of **Schleissheim**, worth visiting because of its palaces and historic aircraft hangar.

The **Old Palace** dates back to the days of Duke Wilhelm V, who had a hermitage built for himself here. Next to it he established a farm, which today is still a state-run estate and a teaching establishment. In 1616 Duke Maximilian I bought the manor Schleissheim from his father for a life annuity and commissioned various artists with the building of a palace. He was fortunate in being able to obtain the services of architect Heinrich Schön, who had already worked at the Munich Residence, and of Peter Candid as an artist for the interior furnishings. In 1623, when Duke Maximilian I was granted the electorate, the residence, built in Italian style, was completed. The Renaissance palace was almost totally destroyed in World War II. The present building dates from the years 1971–2. It is not open to the public.

Schleissheim New Palace

Adjacent to the Old Palace, Elector Maximilian II Emanuel had the ★ **New Palace** built. As early as 1693, Enrico Zuccalli submitted the first plans, in which the New Palace was only to be the eastern end of a four-winged complex also including the Old Palace. The confusion of the War of the Spanish Succession (1704–14) brought the construction to a standstill. It was not until 1719 that Joseph Effner was commissioned to continue the building work. For the interior he engaged, among others, François de Cuvilliés the Elder, and Johann Baptist Zimmermann and Charles Claude Debut, who were responsible for the stucco work. Cosmas Damian Asam, Franz Joachim Bleich and Nikolaus Gottfried Stuber worked on frescoes and paintings. Johann Adam Pichler was responsible for sculptural works. In 1763 Ignaz Günther decorated the wings of the east portal with fine allegorical adornments.

The baroque gallery

The ★ **staircase** was completed in the early 19th century by Leo von Klenze, who had the whole palace redone in a neoclassical style. However, none of these alterations are visible, since the reconstruction after World War II was carried out according to the plans of Joseph Effner. Apart from the artistically decorated rooms, the ★ **baroque gallery** in the New Palace is of particular importance. The picture gallery is part of the Bavarian State Picture Collection and contains works from leading European schools of painting. The Gobelin tapestries, entirely preserved, are of special value too. They were acquired by Elector Maximilian II Emanuel, then governor of the Netherlands, from Flemish manufacturers before 1700.

The eastern counterpart to the New Palace is the ★ **Gartenschloss Lustheim** or Garden Palace Lustheim, built by Enrico Zuccalli in 1684–8 as a wedding gift from Elector Maximilian II Emanuel to his wife Maria Antonia. For the interior frescoes artists like Johann Anton Gumpp, Francesco Rosa and Johann Andreas Trubillio were engaged. Lustheim Palace today houses a ★ collection of Meissen porcelain, donated to the state in 1968 by Ernst Schneider, on the condition that it be displayed only in a baroque setting.

Lustheim

The ★ Park was laid out after 1693; it was in this year that Enrico Zuccalli, having been commissioned to plan the park, toured Holland to study landscape architecture. Dominique Girard, who had earlier had a share in the lay-out of the Nymphenburg Park, was probably decisively involved in the arrangement of this French park as well. The cascade of the canal, extending as far as Lustheim Palace, dates from 1724. Not far from the palaces, on Germany's oldest aerodrome, is the **Historische Flugwerft Schleissheim**, an aircraft hangar that forms a branch of the Deutsches Museum (*see page 25*). Historic aeroplanes and exhibitions on aspects of aviation history and technology can be viewed.

Aircraft Museum exhibit 73

Freising and environs

North of Munich 33km (20 miles) and easily accessible via the road to Freimann or S-Bahn 1, is **Freising** (pop. 30,000). As long ago as the 8th century the bishops St Corbinian, St Boniface and Arbeo lived here. The monastery had its golden age under Bishop Otto von Freising, uncle of Emperor Friedrich I Barbarossa (1152–90). On the hill stands the originally Romanesque ★ **Basilica of St Mary and St Corbinian** (about 1100). The church, with a nave and two aisles, has undergone considerable alterations at various times. The crypt, which contains the shrine of St Corbinian, has completely retained its Romanesque character. The Bestiensäule (beast pillar) is also worth seeing. In 1724 the brothers Asam redid the church with new stucco work and paintings.

Freising

The **Monastery Church Neustift**, north of Freising, was built by Giovanni Antonio Viscardi in 1705–15. The decorations are by Johann Baptist Zimmermann and Franz Xaver Feichtmayr. Ignaz Günther constructed the high altar in 1765. The erstwhile Benedictine Abbey of **Weihenstephan** is now the seat of the agricultural and brewery faculties of Munich Technical University. The brewery, founded in 1146, is the oldest one in the world still in existence. It has a pleasant beer garden.

Art History

Architecture

Although Munich was only founded in 1158, there are a number of structures within the city's present-day boundaries which date back to earlier times. An example is the Romanesque core of the Church of the Holy Cross in Freimann, in the north of the city, which was consecrated as long ago as 815.

The Gothic period is represented by the Frauenkirche, the Altes Rathaus (Old Town Hall) and the Alter Hof (Old Court), the first seat of the Bavarian dukes in Munich. Between 1468 and his death (1488), the town architect Jörg Ganghofer built the Frauenkirche with its *welschen Hauben* (Guelph bonnets), the twin cupolas of the cathedral crowning the towers (one 100m/328ft high, the other 99m/325ft). The church is one of the last late-Gothic hall churches in Germany. Between 1470 and 1474 Ganghofer incorporated parts of an earlier town hall into the Gothic construction of the Altes Rathaus at Marienplatz. The Alter Hof dates from the time of Ludwig the Stern (1253–94). Particularly worthy of note also are the stylistically pure churches in the west part of the city: the Palace Chapel Blutenburg (1488) and the Parish Church of St Wolfgang at Pipping (1478–80).

West facade of the Frauenkirche

75

The Renaissance is represented by three large edifices in Munich: the Münzhof (courtyard of the Mint; 1563–7), surrounded by three-storey arcades, was built by Wilhelm Egkl; Friedrich Sustris was responsible for St Michael's Church (1583–97) and the Maximilian Residence. Between 1569–71 Sustris, together with the Italian Jacobo Strada and Wilhelm Egkl, had the Antiquarium erected. From 1613–16 Sustris worked together with Peter Candid.

Baroque architecture was introduced in Munich under Elector Ferdinand Maria, who laid the foundation for the Theatine Church (St Cajetan); construction was started by the Italian Agostino Barelli and continued by his compatriot Enrico Zuccalli. The church, with its tambour and cupola, gave Munich its first touch of Italian splendour. The Dreifaltigkeitskirche (Trinity Church) was built between 1711 and 1718 by Giovanni Antonio Viscardi. The Asam brothers constructed the famous John Nepomuk Church from 1733 to 1746. St Michael's in Berg am Laim was built by Johann Michael Fischer from 1738 to 1751. Elector Ferdinand Maria allowed Barelli to begin construction on the Nymphenburg Palace in 1664, which his son Maximilian II Emanuel had expanded under Joseph Effner. This architect also finished the New Palace in Schleissheim from 1719 to 1726, a project begun in 1701 by Zuccalli under Maximilian Emanuel's patronage. Zuccalli was earlier reponsible for Lustheim Palace in Schleis-

Sculpture outside St Michael's

sheim (1684–8). The architect, François Cuvilliés, is also connected with Nymphenburg – there he created the Hall of Mirrors and the Amalienburg in true rococo spirit. Another absolute jewel of rococo is the Cuvilliés Theatre in the Residence.

In the 19th century Munich changed from merely a simple city of residence to a true city of art. Ludwig I commissioned the building of the Glyptothek for his collection of classical art and for the Wittelsbach Collection in the Old and New Pinakothek. The National Theatre, originally constructed by Karl von Fischer in 1811 and 1818, was rebuilt after a fire by Leo von Klenze, Ludwig's court architect, between 1823 and 1825. Klenze, along with Friedrich von Gärtner, the sculptor Ludwig Schwanthaler and the painter Peter Cornelius, gave shape to the *Maxvorstadt* (Max suburb), the expansion between Munich and Schwabing, with Ludwigstrasse as the main axis. The Residence received its final form and the Feldherrnhalle and Siegestor were erected. Under Maximilian II, who in his plan to expand the city insisted on consistency with the new style, Maximilianstrasse was laid out. The crowning touch at the end of the street is the Maximilianeum, on the other side of the Isar. The last major expansion of Munich during this period was Prinzregentenstrasse. The patron, Prince Regent Luitpold, used some of Ludwig II's original architectural plans, which had been set aside for lack of funds. The Bavarian National Museum was constructed between 1894 and 1900 by Gabriel von Seidl. Adolf von Hildebrand and Jakob Möhl worked on the Friedensengel (Angel of Peace).

Notable postwar developments include the Olympia Park, which features the Television Tower, the Olympia Hall, the Olympic Stadium, the Olympic Ice-Skating Stadium, and the Olympic Village. Adjacent to this is

The National Theatre

The Maximilianeum

the impressive BMW administrative tower. An eldorado of modern architecture is Arabellapark, a housing and business complex, which is accentuated by the Arabellahaus (1969), the Sheraton Hotel (1971) and most of all the Hypo-Bank Administrative Centre (1981). The so-called postmodern period is represented by the Neue Pinakothek. For months before its completion in 1985, controversy surrounded the plans for the Gasteig Cultural Centre, which, with its broad brickwork facade, now dominates the upper bank of the Isar. Equally controversial was the new Bavarian State Chancellery building, a sweeping horizontal block bordering one side of the Hofgarten. The 1990s will see a number of high-rise projects going up in Munich's north.

The Hypo-Bank building

Sculpture

Gothic influence in sculpture begins to be felt only from about 1400. During the construction of the Frauenkirche, local artists began to make their mark, although at this time and for the following centuries many outside artists were brought to Munich. This was also true of that master of late-Gothic from the Upper Palatinate, Erasmus Grasser (1450–1518), who was commissioned to decorate the Old Town Hall. It was he who sculpted the famous *Moriskentänzer* (Morris Dancers), which once stood in the town hall and are now on display in the city museum.

Although in the Renaissance works of art were produced by native masters like Hans Asslinger or Caspar Weinhart, the most significant pieces of sculpture were made by Italian and Dutch artists. Among the latter was Hubert Gerhard, who designed the statue of Mary on the Mariensäule (St Mary's Column), as well as the Perseus Fountain in the Residence. Hans Krumper was the guiding light in the field of sculpture at the turn of the 17th century. He produced among other things the *Patrona Boiariae* on the west side of the Residence.

In the baroque period Bavarian sculptors were the most prominent, but they had all studied in Italy. A short but representative list must suffice: Tobias Pader, Balthasar Ableithner, Andreas Feistenberger, Egid Quirin Asam, Johann Baptist Straub, Ignaz Günther, and Roman Anton Boos, who made a name for himself in sacred art.

Nineteenth-century Munich sculpture bears the stamp of Ludwig Schwanthaler, a pupil of Bertel Thorvaldsen and Christian Rauch, sculptors brought to Munich by Ludwig I. Schwanthaler created the giant statue of Bavaria at the Theresienwiese, a masterpiece in bronze, cast by Ferdinand von Miller. High perfection in bronze technique is also demonstrated by the Quadriga on top of the Siegestor, a creation of Johann Halbig and Johann Martin von Wagner. At the end of the 19th century Adolf von

Sculptures in wood and stone

Hildebrand was the leading sculptor. Kaspar von Zumbusch and Franz von Stuck were also important.

Painting

The few works from Romanesque times come from anonymous masters. Such is the case in the initial painting from the manuscripts of Emperor Ludwig of Bavaria, done in the Italian style, and the table panel pair (c 1400) representing the *Crucifixion of Christ* and the *Resurrection of Drusiana* (in the Bavarian National Museum).

Painting in Munich reached its first high point in the late-Gothic period. In the second half of the 15th century Jan Polack from Cracow painted the frescoes of St Wolfgang in Pipping, worked on the high altar of the Peterskirche and on the altars of the Palace Chapel Blutenburg. Polack made many designs for windows in the Frauenkirche. Peter Hemmel von Andlau is also famous for his stained-glass windows in the church.

From 1530 onwards, after Munich had stood for some years in the shadow of Nuremberg (Albrecht Dürer) and Regensburg (Albrecht Altdorfer), there developed under Wilhelm IV a court art, the paintings of which provided the basis for the Wittelsbach Collection. Ludwig Reflinger, Hans Burgkmair, Jörg Breu, Melchior Feselen, and Barthel Beham worked on this cycle of historical pictures. Hans Mielich (1516–73) was another important member, who especially excelled in portrait painting. Wilhelm V brought Friedrich Sustris to his court, along with a man from Brügge named de Wit, widely known as Peter Candid.

Johann Heinrich Schönfeld, Joachim von Sandrart, Johann Carl Loth and Johann Andreas Wolff are worthy exponents of the art of the 17th century. Cosmas Damian Asam and Georges Desmarées are the foremost among those connected with the rococo period.

In the 19th century a Munich painting tradition developed, of which Wilhelm von Kobell, Peter von Cornelius, Wilhelm von Kaulbach and Karl von Piloty are regarded as the most famous representatives. Johann Georg von Dillis and Carl Rottmann made names for themselves as landscape painters. Carl Spitzweg concentrated on the idyll of the Bavarian countryside. The leading influences at the end of the 19th century came from Franz von Lenbach, Friedrich August von Kaulbach, Franz von Stuck and Wilhelm Leibl. Characteristic of the early 20th century were the Munich artistic groups. In 1909 Wassily Kandinsky initiated the 'New Artist Group of Munich', which Alexej von Jawlensky, Paul Klee, Alfred Kubin, August Macke, Franz Marc, and Gabriele Münter all joined. Due to differences of opinion the group broke up in 1911 and a new group called *Der Blaue Reiter* (the Blue Rider) gathered around Kandinsky.

Baroque frescoes

Kandinsky's Blaue Reiter

Museums and Collections

Alte Pinakothek, Barer Strasse 27 (north door), tel: 23805216. Daily 10am–5pm, except Monday, Tuesday and Thursday 10am–8pm. Admission charge; Sunday and public holidays free (*see page 46*).

Neue Pinakothek, Barer Strasse 29 (entrance Theresienstrasse), tel: 23805/195. Daily 10am–5pm, except Monday, Tuesday and Thursday 10am–8pm. Admission charge; Sunday and public holidays free (*see page 48*).

Staatsgalerie moderner Kunst (State Gallery of Modern Art), Prinzregentenstrasse 1, tel: 292710. Daily except Monday 10am–5pm , Thursday also until 10pm. Admission charge; Sunday and public holidays free (*see page 53*).

Schackgalerie, Prinzregentenstrasse 9, tel: 23805/224. Daily 9.15am–4.30pm except Tuesday. Admission charge; Sunday and public holidays free (*see page 57*).

Staatliche Antikensammlungen (Collection of Classical Art), Königsplatz 1, tel: 598359. Daily 10am–5pm, except Monday, Tuesday and Thursday 10am–8pm. Admission charge (*see page 45*).

Attic vases in the Collection of Classical Art

Glyptothek, Königsplatz 3, tel: 286100. Daily 10am–5pm, except Monday, Tuesday and Thursday 10am–8pm. Admission charge (*see page 45*).

Glyptothek exhibit

Schatzkammer der Residenz (The Royal Treasury), Max-Joseph-Platz 3, tel: 290671. Daily 10am–4.30pm except Monday. Admission charge (*see page 31*).

Residenzmuseum, Max-Joseph-Platz 3, tel: 290671. Daily 10am–4.30pm except Monday. It includes the famous Cuvilliés Theatre. Weekdays 2–5pm, Sunday 10am–5pm. Admission charge (*see page 31*).

Staatliche Graphische Sammlung (State Collection of the Graphic Arts), Meiserstrasse 10, tel: 5591/490. Monday to Thursday 10am–1pm, Monday to Wednesday also 2–4.30pm, Thursday 2–6pm, Friday 10am–12.30pm. Admission free (*see page 44*).

Staatliche Sammlung Ägyptischer Kunst (State Collection of Egyptian Art), Hofgartenstrasse 1, tel: 298546. Tuesday to Friday 9am–4pm, Tuesday also 7–9pm, Saturday and Sunday 10am–5pm. Admission charge; Sunday and public holidays free (*see page 34*).

Staatliche Münzsammlung (State Collection of Coins), Residenzstrasse 1, tel: 227221. Daily except Monday 10am–4.30pm. Admission charge; Sunday and public holidays free.

Staatliches Museum für Völkerkunde (State Ethnological Museum) Maximilianstrasse 42, tel: 2285506. Daily 10am–5pm except Monday. Admission charge (*see page 51*).

Bayerisches Nationalmuseum (Bavarian National

Museum) Prinzregentenstrasse 3, tel: 21680. Daily except Monday 9.30am–4.30pm. Some sections are closed during lunchtime. Admission charge; Sunday and public holidays free (*see page 55*).

Die Neue Sammlung (The New Collection), Prinzregentenstrasse 3, tel: 227844. Daily 10am–5pm except Monday. Admission charge.

Prähistorische Staatssammlung (Prehistoric State Collection), Lerchenfeldstrasse 2, tel: 293911. Daily 9.30am–4pm except Monday, Thursday until 8pm. Admission charge; Sunday and public holidays free (*see page 56*).

Burgmuseum Grünwald, Zeillerstrasse 3, tel: 6413218. Wednesday to Sunday 10am–4.30pm. Closed December–mid-March. Admission charge (*see page 69*).

Städtische Galerie im Lenbachhaus (Municipal Gallery), Luisenstrasse 33, tel: 521041. Daily 10am–6pm except Monday. Admission charge; Sunday and public holidays free (*see page 46*).

From the Puppet Theatre Collection

Münchner Stadtmuseum (Municipal Museum), Sankt-Jakobs-Platz 1, tel: 233/2370. Daily 9am–4.30pm except Monday, Sunday and public holidays 10am–6pm. Admission charge; Sunday and public holidays free. The museum also houses a collection of musical instruments, the photographic and film museum, the museum of fashion (Modemuseum), a museum on home décor and a puppet theatre collection (*see page 20*).

Lunar landing

Deutsches Museum, on the Isarinsel (island), tel: 21791. Daily 9am–5pm. Admission charge (*see page 25*).

Deutsches Jagd- und Fischereimuseum (German Hunting and Fishing Museum), Neuhauser Strasse 53, tel: 220522. Daily 9.30am–5pm and Thursday 9.30am–9pm. Admission charge (*see page 15*).

Jüdisches Museum München (Jewish Museum), Maximilianstrasse 36, tel: 297453. Tuesday and Wednesday 2–6pm, Thursday 2–8pm. Admission free.

Mineralogische Staatssammlung (State Collection of Mineralogy), Theresienstrasse 41 (entrance Barer Strasse), tel: 2394-1. Daily 10am–6pm except Monday for special exhibitions. Admission charge.

BMW Museum, Petuelring 130 (opposite the Olympia Park), tel: 38953307. Daily 9am–5pm. Admission charge (*see page 62*).

Siemens Museum, Prannerstrasse 10, tel: 234/2660. Monday to Saturday 9am–5pm, Sunday 10am–5pm; the first Tuesday of every month open until 9pm. Admission free.

Valentin Musäum, Tower of Isartor, tel: 223266. Monday, Tuesday, Friday, Saturday 11.01am–5.29pm, Sunday 10.01am–5.29pm. Admission charge (*see page 25*). Karl Valentin was a popular Munich folk comedian.

Music and Theatre

In 1482 a church choir was founded in Munich and musical life in this period was influenced by the blind organist and composer Konrad Paumann. In 1526 the Swiss musician Ludwig Senfl became leader of the court orchestra, and from 1556 till 1594 this position was held by Orlando di Lasso, one of the great figures of Renaissance music.

In the 17th century the Italian opera was established in Munich. In the 18th century Mozart tried without success to enter the service of the court. His operas *Tristan and Isolde* and *Idomeneo* were first performed in Munich, but were treated harshly by the critics.

In the second half of the 19th century under Ludwig II, the Munich opera, along with Bayreuth, became the bearer of the artistic ideas of Richard Wagner. In 1901 Max Reger left the Upper Palatinate to come to Munich. Hans Pfitzner taught from 1929 onwards at the Akademie der Tonkunst (Academy of Musical Art). Richard Strauss was Munich's 'great son'. After World War II the music scene was dominated by Carl Orff, Werner Egk and Karl Amadeus Hartmann.

With such traditions, it is hardly surprising that Munich remains conservative in cultural matters. Contemporary artists chafe at the city's emphasis on its venerable cultural establishments. The Bavarian State Opera, the State Playhouse, and the Munich Philharmonic receive generous financial support from the government; smaller ensembles have to struggle to survive. This means that Munich is a great city in which to hear or see traditional German art.

Concerts

Concerts take place primarily in the **Herkulessaal** in the Residence, in the **Grosser Sendesaal** des Bayerischen Rundfunks (concert hall of the Bavarian Broadcasting Corporation), in the **Olympiahalle** (pop concerts), in the **Hochschule für Musik** (Music Academy, Arcisstrasse 12) as well as in the Kleiner Konzertsaal, Philharmonic Hall and Carl-Orff-Saal at **Gasteig** Culture Centre. Advance booking Monday to Friday 10.30am–2pm and 3–6pm, Saturday 10.30am–2pm, tel: 48098614.

Gasteig Culture Centre

Munich has three large symphony orchestras: Bavarian State Orchestra, Munich Philharmonic and the Bavarian Radio Orchestra. In addition to the Münchner Kammerorchester, there are also many other chamber music groups. Good jazz can be heard at **Unterfahrt** (Kirchenstrasse 96) and **Allotria** (Oskar-von-Miller-Ring 3).

Opera and ballet

As an art form, opera is given greater priority in Germany than in any other country in the world and a German city's opera house is an expression of civic pride. This is especially true of Munich with its completely renovated National Theatre:

National Theatre performance

Nationaltheater, Max-Joseph-Platz. Advance booking only at Maximilianstrasse 11, tel: 221316. Box office hours Monday to Friday 10am–1pm and 3.30–5.30pm, Saturday 10am–12.30pm.

Operetta

Staatstheater am Gärtnerplatz, Gärtnerplatz, tel: 201-6767. Box office hours Monday to Friday 10am–12.30pm and 3.30–5.30pm, Saturday 10am–12.30pm. Also one hour before performances. In addition to popular operettas and musicals, operas are also performed here.

Theatres

Altes Residenztheater (Cuvilliés Theatre), in the Residence. Entrance Residenzstrasse, tel: 221316. Advance booking as for Nationaltheater. Operas and plays suitable to this, the most beautiful rococo theatre in the world, are performed here, also *Lieder* matinées and chamber music concerts.

Residenztheater, Max-Joseph-Platz 1, tel: 225754. Box office hours Monday to Friday 10am–1pm. and 3.30–5.30pm, Saturday 10am–12.30pm.

Prinzregententheater, Prinzregentenplatz 12, tel: 221315. Advance booking as for Nationaltheater. Classical and modern dramas.

Deutsches Theater, Schwanthalerstrasse 13, tel: 514 4360. Advance booking Monday to Friday noon–6pm, Saturday 10am–1.30pm. Revues, musicals, international guest performances.

Münchner Kammerspiele, in the Schauspielhaus (Playhouse), Maximilianstrasse 26, tel: 2372/1328. Advance booking Monday to Friday 10am–6pm, Saturday, Sunday and public holidays 10am–1pm. Classical and modern dramas.

Theater im Marstall, Marstallplatz, tel: 225754. Advance booking Monday to Friday 10am–1pm and 3.30–5.30pm, Saturday 10am–12.30pm. Experimental theatre performances of the State Opera and the Residenztheater.

Werkraumtheater der Münchner Kammerspiele, Hildegardstrasse 1, tel: 2372 1328. Advance booking as for Kammmerspiele. Stage for avant-garde theatre.

Komödie im Bayerischen Hof, in the Bayerischer Hof, Promenadeplatz, tel: 292810. Advance booking Monday to Saturday 11am–6pm.

Komödie am Max-II, Maximilianstrasse 47, tel: 221-859. Advance booking Monday to Saturday 11am–8pm, Sunday and public holidays 3–8pm.

Münchner Volkstheater, Brienner Strasse 50, tel: 5234655. Advance booking Monday to Friday 10am–1pm and 3–6pm, Saturday 10am–1pm and 5–6.30pm, Sunday 5–6.30pm. Folk plays.

Theater 'Kleine Freiheit', Maximilianstrasse 31, tel: 221123. Advance booking Monday to Saturday from 11am, Sunday from 3pm. Boulevard theatre.

Modernes Theater, Hans-Sachs-Strasse 12, tel: 266821. Advance booking, tel: 225473. Daily except Monday. Avant-garde theatre.

Theater im Karlshof, Karlstrasse 43. Advance booking, tel: 59661. Daily from 11am–1pm and from 5–7pm. Boulevard plays, shows.

Teamtheater and Teamtheater Tankstelle, Am Einlass 4–5 and 2a, tel: 2604333. Advance booking Monday to Friday 10am–5pm. At the box office from 6pm. Works by modern playwrights and new interpretations of the classics.

Theater 44, Hohenzollernstrasse 20. Advance booking by telephone from 4pm, tel: 3228748. Daily except Sunday and Monday. Modern drama.

Theater im Fraunhofer, Fraunhoferstrasse 9, tel: 266460. Advance booking Monday–Friday 2–6pm. Modern English-language drama often performed.

TamS, Haimhauser Strasse 13a, tel: 345890. Advance booking on performance days from 4pm, Friday, Saturday, Sunday. Mostly modern plays, sometimes in local Bavarian dialect.

Theater Scaramouche, Hesseloher Strasse 3. Advance booking by telephone from 3pm, tel: 334555. Contemporary theatre, popular plays, songs and revues.

Blutenburgtheater, Blutenburgstrasse 35, tel: 1234300. Ticket office 5–8pm. Famous for its crime and detective plays.

Schauburg in der Au, Theater der Jugend, Konradinstrasse 7, tel: 2372/1365. Advance booking Monday to Friday 9am–5.30pm, Saturday 1.30–5.30pm.

Münchner Theater für Kinder, Dachauer Strasse 46, tel: 595454/593858. Advance bookings: open daily 10am–5.30pm.

Münchner Marionettentheater, Blumenstrasse 29a, tel: 265712. Advance booking Tuesday to Sunday 10am–12pm. Puppet theatre.

Children's Theatre poster

Cabaret

Münchner Lach- und Schiessgesellschaft, Haimhauserstrasse/corner Ursulastrasse, tel: 391997. Advance booking daily from 2pm. Political cabaret.

Novaks Schwabinger Brettl, Occamstrasse 11, tel: 347289. International cabaret in the atmosphere of old Schwabing.

On parade

Annual Events

Fasching. The Munich calendar opens with the pre-Lenten carnival known locally as *Fasching* (**7 January until Ash Wednesday**). This period of unrestrained merriment has the same origin as the Rhenish carnival, but is probably based on pre-Christian festivals greeting the return of spring. Masquerades, glitter, and flirting are trumps. The artists' parties in Schwabing are particularly outstanding, as well as the activities of *Fasching* organisations, press and film balls, and the dances of the *Damische Ritter* – the 'daft knights' – or the *Vorstadthochzeit* – the 'suburban wedding'. On Fasching Sunday, the Sunday before Ash Wednesday, the theme is 'Foolish Munich'. In the afternoon a great public festival takes place between Marienplatz and Karlstor. On Fasching Tuesday (Shrove Tuesday) the market women dance at the Viktualienmarkt in the morning, while in the afternoon there is unrestrained activity all through the central city.

Starkbierzeit (the strong beer season). This begins in **March** (around St Joseph's Day, 19 March). The Munich breweries serve a special kind of brown beer in a strictly observed ceremony. This beer has a maximum alcohol content of six percent. The most popular centres of attraction are the Salvatorkeller on the Nockherberg in the district of Giesing, and the Löwenbräukeller at the beginning of Nymphenburgerstrasse.

Biennale. Biennial international festival for new music theatre (end of **April/May**).

Auer Dult. This market and fair, which takes place three times a year, in spring, summer and autumn, is held at Mariahilfplatz in the Au quarter. In addition to the usual pleasures like roundabouts, there is also a flea market.

Contentment in a beer tent

Maibock (or May beer). Consumption of this pure and

somewhat lighter brown beer without additional coloured malt brings the Starkbierzeit to a close. Originally Maibock came from northern Germany, to be exact from Einbeck in Lower Saxony. Duke Wilhelm V, who founded the Hofbräuhaus in 1589, had his master brewer brought from there. In 1614 Elias Pichler presented this drink for the first time, and its sale was a special privilege of the court until 1818. The testing of the Maibock (around the end of April) is regarded as an 'official act of state'.

Fronleichnam (Corpus Christi). The Roman Catholic Corpus Christi procession on the second Thursday after Whitsun is a particularly magnificent demonstration in Munich. It traditionally begins at 8am with a communal religious service at Marienplatz.

Münchner Musiksommer (Munich Music Summer). Munich Philharmonic performances (**June/July**).

Filmfest München (Munich Film Festival, last week of **June**) at selected cinemas and Gasteig Culture Centre.

Summer Festival (**July and August**). At the centre of the so-called 'Festive Summer' is the Opera Festival with conductors and singers of international reputation at the National Theatre. Concerts in the Nymphenburg Palace, the Ballet Week Festival, Lieder recitals, evenings in the Herkulessaal and matinées in the Cuvilliés Theatre, as well as concerts in the Brunnenhof of the Residence round out this highlight of musical life.

Oktoberfest (middle of **September** until first Sunday in **October**). A horse race at the wedding of Crown Prince Ludwig (later King Ludwig I) to Princess Therese von Sachsen-Hildburghausen in 1810 signalled the birth of the present giant fair. Until well into the middle of the 19th century horse races and shooting contests remained highlights of the festival. But since that time the more popular attractions such as roller coasters, Ferris wheels, and the house of horrors, etc have become increasingly prevalent. Today the *Wies'n*, as the Munich citizens call their popular festival at the Theresienwiese, attracts well over six million people per year, who drink more than 5.5 million litres (1½ million gallons) of beer during the sixteen days of the festival. The Oktoberfest begins when the mayor taps the first barrel of beer. The main attractions are the opening procession of *Wies'n* brewers and innkeepers with their splendidly decorated beer wagons followed by the one carrying the Festival Queen, and the great Bavarian costume parade on the first Sunday, which includes groups from various nationalities.

The Oktoberfest

Christkindlmarkt (the three weeks before Christmas). Goods are sold at Marienplatz and the connecting streets of the pedestrian zone. Additional markets are held at Münchner Freiheit, Weissenburger Platz, Rotkreuzplatz and the Chinese Tower in the English Garden.

Food and Drink

The Munich cuisine is based on that of Upper Bavaria. Influences from Tyrol, Bohemia, Franconia and Swabia are traceable in the local fare.

Specialities

A magic word for Munich cooking is *Brotzeit*. It can be taken at any hour of the day, and is best translated as 'snack'. A *Brotzeit* might consist of *Leberkäs*, a unique kind of meat loaf which contains neither liver nor cheese. This baked mixture of minced beef and pork, spiced with marjoram and nutmeg, can be eaten hot or cold at one of the city's countless *Imbisstube*. The famous *Weisswürste* (white sausages) are made out of veal and parsley. They are spiced with sweet mustard and eaten with *Brezen* (pretzels). *Weisswürste* are not allowed to hear the bell strike 12 o'clock, which means they should be eaten only before noon. The rather less filling *Wurstsalat* incorporates slices of a particular kind of cold sausage (*Leoner*) with a lot of onion rings, vinegar, oil and pepper.

As far as typical main meals are concerned, Bavaria is famous for its hearty fare. Nowhere is this better displayed than in the ubiquitous *Schweinebraten mit Blaukraut und Knödel* – roast pork with red cabbage and dumpling. Dumplings come in two varieties: *Semmelknödel*, made of bread crumbs, and *Kartoffelknödel*, made of grated potatoes. For real pork fans, *Schweinshax'n* – pork knuckles – are as Bavarian as it gets. Mention should also be made of the distinctive Upper Bavarian *Saure Lüngerl*, lung prepared in a special manner in a vinegar sauce, which also comes with *Semmelknödel*.

Beer gardens have their own specialities. You'll find *Hax'n* aplenty, as well as roast chicken (*Hendl*); *Rippchen* (spare ribs) are also popular. Giant *Brezen* are a treat; if you want to be really Bavarian, smear them with *Obazda*, an orangey cheese spread made with Camembert, onion, paprika, caraway, egg yolk and butter; sometimes *Gervais* is used as the basic ingredient. You may notice people eating something that looks like paper: these are *Radi*, thinly sliced white radishes. To enjoy these properly, salt them and wait a few minutes to let them 'weep', taking away their sharpness.

Traditional Munich restaurants

Alter Wirt, Grünwald, Marktplatz 1, tel: 6419340. Daily 7am–midnight. Rustic elegance, not cheap.

Augustiner Gastätten, Neuhauser Strasse 16, tel: 23183257. Daily 9am–midnight. Traditional Bavarian fare in real Munich atmosphere in the pedestrian precinct.

Boettner, Theatinerstrasse 8, tel: 221210. Monday to

87

The ubiquitous Semmelknödel

Zur Hundskugel Restaurant

Weissbier and Brezen

Friday 11am–midnight, Sunday 11am–3pm. French and regional cuisine, only the best ingredients, and corresponding prices.

Donisl, Weinstrasse 1, tel: 220184. Daily 9am–1am. Bavarian specialities consumed in the old Munich atmosphere right on Marienplatz.

Halali, Schönfeldstrasse 22, tel: 285909. Closed for Saturday lunch, Sunday and public holidays. Traditional Munich venue.

Haxnbauer, Münzstrasse 5, tel: 29162100. Daily 11am–1am. Old Bavarian inn where the shanks are turned over open beech wood fires.

Hundskugel, Hotterstrasse 18, tel: 264272. Daily 10am–1am. Munich's oldest inn, first mentioned in 1440.

Nürnberger Bratwurstglöckl, Frauenplatz 9, tel: 220385. Daily 9am–midnight. The best Nürnberger Schweinswürste (pork sausages) are grilled over a beech wood fire.

Ratskeller, Marienplatz 8, tel: 2199890. Daily 9am–midnight. One of the biggest of Munich's cellar restaurants in the catacombs of the town hall.

Straubinger Hof, Blumenstrasse 5, tel: 2608444. Daily 9am–11pm except weekends and public holidays. Traditional Bavarian home cooking.

Weinhaus Neuner, Herzogspitalstrasse 8, tel: 2603954. Daily 5pm–1am except Sunday. Reservations advisable. Regional cuisine, combined with French *nouvelle cuisine*.

Weinstadl, Burgstrasse 6, tel: 221047. Monday to Saturday 10am–11.30pm, Sunday and public holidays 4pm–midnight. The oldest house in Munich where the late-Gothic pillars have been preserved.

Weisses Bräuhaus, Tal 10, tel: 4316381. Large restaurant in the centre of the town, with an enormous selection of Bavarian dishes. Famous for its dark *Weissbier* (Aventinus) brewed by the Schneider brewery.

Wurstkuchl, Amalienstrasse 87, tel: 7854622. Daily 10am–12.30am. Simple dishes and home-made sausages.

Zum Spöckmeier am Roseneck, Rosenstrasse 9, tel: 268088. Daily 9am–midnight, Sunday 9am–5pm. Traditional old Munich inn, where people meet to eat *Weisswurst* in the morning.

Gourmet restaurants

Munich also has a good variety of gourmet restaurants which serve some of the most exquisite, if expensive, cuisine in Germany.

Am Glockenbach, Kapuzinerstrasse 29, tel: 534043. Daily noon–2pm and 7pm–1am. French and Bavarian cuisine in intimate drawing room atmosphere. Certainly one of the best restaurants in the city.

Grüne Gans, Munich 5, Am Einlass 5, tel: 266228. Daily except Saturday evenings. Intimate Munich gourmets' meeting place.

Käfer-Schänke, Schumannstrasse 1, tel: 4168-0. Closed on Sunday and public holidays. Hidden behind the gourmet shop are a number of elegant rooms where one may dine undisturbed.

Le Gourmet/Schwarzwälder, Mannstrasse 8, tel: 227216. Open evenings only except Sunday. Special regional cuisine offered by Otto Koch.

Le Cezanne, Konradstrasse 1, tel: 391805. The master chef Joel Noguier conjures delicacies for the palate at prices within reach.

Tantris, Johann-Fichte-Strasse 7, tel: 362061. Open Tuesday to Friday noon–3pm and 6.30–10.30pm. The second top restaurant in Munich, managed by Hans Haas.

Munich beer

The main drink in Munich and throughout Bavaria is still beer. Protected by the oldest food law, Duke William's purity law of 1516, which forbids the use of anything but water, barley and hops in brewing, Bavarian beer is still made today from natural products without any chemical additives. The light and dark draught beer (lager) has a *wort* of 11–12 percent, *Märzenbier* has 13–14 percent. During certain times of the year *Bock* beer is brewed, with a *wort* of 18–19 percent.

A special kind of beer is *Weissbier*, a light, slightly sparkling beer made from wheat instead of barley. Since 1977 the Bavarian Alt beer has been brewed again. The measure for beer is the *Mass*, which is about one litre (1¼ pint), half of this is *eine Halbe*. In beer gardens, most beer is served in *Masskrüge*.

Beer halls and gardens

Augustinerkeller, Arnulfstrasse 52, tel: 594393. Daily 10am–1am. Apart from the restaurant there is a beer garden seating 5,000 with self service, snack stalls and sometimes a brass band.

Bräustüberl der Forschungsbrauerei, Unterhachinger Strasse 76, tel: 6701169. Tuesday to Saturday 11am–11pm, Sunday 10am–11pm. Bavarian sausage specialities in the original brewery with a large garden.

Chinesischer Turm, Englischer Garten, tel: 3838730. In good weather 11am–1am. Every visitor to Munich must come here. It has 7,000 seats and is all self service.

Flaucher, Isarauen 1, tel: 7232677. Daily 10am–11pm. A place to make a trip to, next to the river Isar. One of Munich's best beer gardens with reasonable prices.

Hackerkeller, Theresienhöhe 4, tel: 507004. Daily 5pm–1am. Ox on the spit is the speciality of the house.

Headgear for a horse

A relaxing pastime

Hofbräuhaus am Platzl, Am Platzl, tel: 221676. Daily 9am–midnight. This must be one of the most famous pubs in the world.

Hofbräukeller, Innere Wiener Strasse 19, tel: 4599250. Daily 8.30am–midnight. A popular venue for beer garden connoisseurs.

Hirschgarten, Hirschgartenalle 1, tel: 172591. November to February daily 11.30am–10pm; closed Tuesday. Munich's largest beer garden, seating 8,000, with adjoining game enclosure.

Hirschau, Gysslingstrasse 7, tel: 369942. Always open in good weather, restaurant closed on Monday. Children's playground, which can be conveniently supervised from the beer tables.

Löwenbräu-Keller, Nymphenburgerstrasse 2, tel: 526021. Daily 9am–midnight. Traditional Munich beer cellar in the heart of the city.

Mathäser Bierstadt, Bayerstrasse 5, tel: 3132519. Daily bar 8am–midnight; restaurant 10.30am–midnight. This typical Munich beer cellar has over 4,500 seats, and thus is by far the largest pub in the world.

Max-Emanuel-Brauerei, Adalbertstrasse 33, tel: 2715158. Daily 10am–1am. Famous not only for the folk music performances, but also for the 'White Festivals' at carnival, and for its jazz concerts.

Menterschweige, Harthauser Strasse 70, tel: 640732. Daily 11am–midnight. Reservation requested (in the restaurant). This lovely restaurant has long catered to people making excursions on the bank of the Isar.

Osterwaldgarten, Keferstrasse 12, tel: 38405040. Daily 11am–1am. Old Schwabing beer garden with ancient chestnut trees.

Pschorr-Keller, Theresienhöhe 7, tel: 501088. Daily 8am–midnight. A typical Munich beer hall (total 3,500 seats, beer garden 600) with music by a quartet, and grilled suckling pig.

Salvator-Keller, Munich 90, Hochstrasse, tel: 4599130. Daily 9am–11pm. One of the beer centres of Munich (seating 2,000 inside and 3,000 in the beer garden). Good bourgeois cuisine, good value for money.

Waldwirtschaft Grosshesselohe, Grosshesselohe, Georg-Kalb-Strasse 3, tel: 74994030. Beer garden daily. Restaurant 10.30am–11.30pm except Monday and Tuesday. Well known particularly by jazz fans.

Zum Aumeister, Munich 45, Sondermeierstrasse 9, tel: 325224. Daily 8am–11pm except Monday. Favourite excursion destination, on the northern edge of the English Garden (beer garden has 2,500 seats).

Unionsbräu, Einsteinstr. 42, tel: 477677. Daily 11am–1am. One of the traditional, rustic beer cellars of Munich with restaurant and own small brewery.

Nightlife

Cinemas

There are numerous cinemas all over Munich. The main 'art film' cinemas recommended are Theatiner-Film in Theatinerstrasse, Isabella in Neureutherstrasse, Türkendolch and Neues Arri in Türkenstrasse, Lupe 2 in Ungererstrasse, and Neues Rottmann in Rottmannstrasse. Germany's first IMAX cinema is contained in the Forum of Technology on the Museum Island. English-language films can be seen at the Cinema at Nymphenburgerstrasse 31 and the Museum Lichtspiele at the eastern end of the Ludwigsbrücke.

Late Night

Beer gardens close at 10pm, and most other Munich establishments shut their doors by 1am. Anyone who wants a night out on the town here has to work a little harder than in other cities. However, there are an increasing number of establishments where you can eat, drink and dance the night away, in surroundings for every taste and to suit every wallet.

A night-time venue

Bars

Atomic Café. Neuturmstr. 5. Lively meeting place for 1970s fans, with cocktail bar and dance floor.

Harry's New York Bar, Falkenturmstr. 9. 4pm–3am, closed Sunday. Distinguished, with piano music.

Iwan, Josephspitalstr. 18. 11pm–3am. For stylish, liberal city slickers, who have no financial worries; very popular with the gay crowd.

Nachtcafé, Maximiliansplatz 5. 7pm–5am. Only really gets going after midnight. Unobtrusive live jazz music, mixed clientele, quite cosmopolitan: food is cooked right through the night.

Schumann's, Maximilianstr. 36. 5pm–3am. Elite and exclusive reputation, more for VIPs than vamps.

Discos and clubs

Bongo Bar, Grafinger Str. 6. 1920s-style nightclub, concentrating mainly on chanson, with more arty and erotic shows on Friday and Saturday nights.

Babalu, Leopoldstr. 19. Exclusive establishment geared to the younger crowd.

P 1, Prinzregentenstr.1. 10pm–4am. Situated in the basement of the Haus der Kunst; the place to go for jet-setters and celebrities.

Kunstpark Ost. Giant disco and club complex near the Ostbahnhof. Each hall geared to a different theme and including: Babylon, Raving, HipHop, House and Blackbeat, as well as Natraj Tempel and Psychedelic Trance.

A city of elegance...

Shopping

As a city of art, fashion and fairs, Munich of course has a wide range of shops, which provide a choice of goods.

Fashion

Some of the world's most elegant fashion houses have branches in Munich. Not only Bavarian folk costume but also the most extravagant new trends are to be found – especially in the attractive boutiques of Schwabing.

For the particularly fastidious taste the fashion shops of Maximilianstrasse are recommended. Bagheera, TAP, Guy Laroche, Lothar's and St Laurent, among others, have branches there. But there are also old-established fashion stores like English House, Rudolph Moshammer, or Unützer, which sell elegant and sporty outfits.

Genuine elegance is offered in Theatinerstrasse (Eckerle-Moden, Maendler, Rodier), in Perusastrasse (Otto Weller), in Residenzstrasse (Max Dietl, Daniel Hechter, Ponater-Modelle), in Brienner Strasse (E Braun), at Amiraplatz (Ted Lapidus, Missoni) and at Promenadeplatz (Rudolph Moshammer, Emilio Pucci).

92

...and tradition

Bavarian style clothing can be purchased at Loden-Frey (Maffeistrasse, the largest special store for *loden* cloth and national costume in the world), Dirndl-Königin (Residenzstrasse), Wallach (Residenzstrasse). Other outlets include Die Schöne Münchnerin (Petersplatz), Salzburger Trachtenstube (Neuhauser Strasse), Trachtenalm (Herzogspitalstrasse) and Zugspitz-Moden (Bahnhofsplatz, Neuhauser and Sendlinger Strasse).

Lower-priced stores at Marienplatz (Beck), in Rosenstrasse (Fischer), in Kaufingerstrasse (Arendt), in Neuhauser Strasse (Stalf, Haus der Mode, Lacher), as well as in Sendlinger Strasse.

Big department stores are located mainly in the pedestrian zones (Kaufinger-, Neuhauser- and Schützenstrasse), and at Karlsplatz. Boutiques can be found especially in Schwabing in Türkenstrasse, Amalienstrasse, Leopoldstrasse, and Hohenzollernstrasse.

Shoe stores for elegant and extravagant tastes are located in Theatiner-, Perusa- and Maximilianstrasse.

Art shops

The art trade is centred in Maximilianstrasse, in Briennerstrasse, Theatinerstrasse and in the Ottoblock in Ottostrasse, as well as in many smaller galleries in the arcades of the Hofgarten and in Schwabing (Türkenstrasse).

Antiques

Valuable (and expensive) antiques are offered in the shops on Fürstenstrasse and Neuturmstrasse. All over Schwabing (especially in Barer Strasse and Türkenstrasse) there are shops specialising in 'English antiques', silver, glass, *Jugendstil* (art nouveau), or art deco. At Antic-Haus (Neuturmstrasse 1) several dealers have set up a mutual undertaking in a huge area. In addition, there are many smaller antique shops grouped around Viktualienmarkt. Every year in autumn the German Art and Antique Fair takes place at the Haus der Kunst. In addition, there are several smaller antique fairs at the Deutsches Museum and the Pschorr-Keller.

Furnishings and arts and crafts

Modern fittings

Furnishing of quality is offered by stores in Brienner Strasse (eg Beringer und Koettgen). The big furniture stores are located in the street Tal. Haus Bernheimer at Promenadeplatz specialises in furnishings, art, and antiques. The Kunstgewerbe-Verein in Pacellistrasse is known for arts and crafts, in particular Bavarian articles, but there are also numerous shops in Theatiner- and Maximilianstrasse. In Maximilianstrasse there are no fewer than 25 galleries to browse through, and to spend in.

93

Bookshops
As a great publishing city, Munich has a wide variety of bookshops, especially in the city centre. Situated directly opposite the Town Hall on Marienplatz, Hugendubel has a vast collection of books spread out over its three floors. English books can be bought at Anglia at Schellingstrasse 3 and at Words' Worth at Schellingstrasse 21a.

A popular souvenir

Foodhalls
Try the foodhalls of the Kaufhof department store at Stacchus or on Marienplatz, as well as that of Hertie on Bahnhofsplatz. For a selection of the finest delicatessen, there is Käfer on Prinzregentenstrasse and Dallmayer behind the town hall. The latter, with its indoor fountain, is a veritable temple of fine food and drink, selling both international and regional specialities.

Markets
Munich's most famous open-air market for foodstuffs is the Viktualienmarkt in the city centre, very close to Marienplatz. Other permanent markets for produce include the Haidhauser Markt (Wienerplatz), the Pasinger Viktualienmarkt (Bäckerstrasse) and the Schwabinger Markt (Elisabethplatz).

Getting There

By air

There are numerous direct flights to Munich from both the UK and the US. Munich's new international airport is located 28km (17 miles) north of the city near Erding. From the airport the quickest means of reaching the city is by the S-Bahn (suburban train), which leaves the terminal every 20 minutes from 3.55am–12.55am and costs DM13.20 for adults (eight stripes on a blue multiple-journey ticket. You may consider buying a day-ticket covering the whole Munich transport system area (*see page 97*).

There is also the Airport Shuttle bus which runs every 20 minutes between the main station (Hauptbahnhof) and the airport terminal. It costs DM15 one way. The other alternative is to take a taxi, which costs around DM120.

By train

Munich is easily accessible from all major cities in Europe. The main station, with a wide choice of hotels in the vicinity, is not far from Stachus and the pedestrian precinct, and has very good S-Bahn (suburban rail), U-Bahn (underground), tram and taxi connections.

The German Railways information centre has all the important information, timetables, etc you'll need (daily 8am–10pm, summer season 8am–11pm). There are some important telephone numbers for train connections which those travelling by train should take note of:

Hannover–Hamburg and Bremen, tel: 11531.
Austria and Southern Europe, tel: 11532.
Tyrol, Italy, Switzerland, tel: 11533.
Cologne, Dortmund, Paris, Holland, Belgium, tel: 11534.

By car

Munich is well served by motorways coming in from all directions. They all converge on the Middle Ring Road (Mittlerer Ring). The A9 comes down from the north (Berlin–Würzburg–Nuremberg); the A8 from the southeast (Salzburg) and the west (Stuttgart–Ulm); the A95 from the south (Garmisch) and the A96 from the southwest (Lindau–Landsberg).

Car-piloting services (which also provide round-the-clock information about hotels) are available on Autobahn exits. An hour of car-piloting service with passenger guide costs DM29, with guide driving ahead DM32. Car-piloting stations are in Freimann (Autobahn Nürnberg, tel: 325-417), Obermenzing (Autobahn Stuttgart, tel: 8112412) and Ramersdorf (Autobahn Salzburg, tel: 672755). Further motorists' services include: ADAC Information, tel: 505061; ADAC breakdown service, tel: 19211; ACE Auto Club Europa eV emergency service, tel: 536502

Getting Around

Parking

Munich is about to suffocate in traffic, and finding a parking space is like winning a lottery. Leave your car where you're staying or outside town, and use the excellent system of public transport, take a taxi or walk. There are two car parks in the city centre in case you can't do without: at Stachus (entrance via Sonnen/Bayerstrasse), Monday to Friday 7am–midnight, Sunday and public holidays 1pm–midnight; and at Färbergraben (entrance via Herzogspitalstrasse), Monday to Friday 7am–midnight, closed Sunday and public holidays.

Public Transport

Public transport is amalgamated in the so-called Münchner Verkehrs- und Tarifverbund (MVV). A properly stamped ticket (*see page 97*) is good for the immediate area on all S- and U-Bahn trains, trams and buses.

The most laid back method of transport is the tram; trams continue to ply their way through the city centre and, as well as getting you from A to B, they provide you with an excellent chance of some relaxing sightseeing.

The U-Bahn (underground) is the fast way of getting around central Munich. It's a direct offspring of Munich's rise in status to Olympic City in 1972, and has been extended constantly ever since.

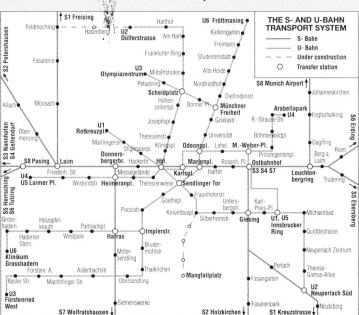

The S-Bahn (suburban rail) lines serve thousands of commuters within a 40-km (25-mile) radius, and are an excellent means of getting beyond the city limits into some of the surrounding countryside.

The blue-and-white Munich buses provide a fill-in network for points not directly served by the underground or trams.

Tickets and fares

While the system itself works very efficiently, knowing which tickets to buy for which zones can take some getting used to.

Tickets (single-journey or strip tickets) can either be obtained from automatic ticket machines at the stations or stops, or from newsagents with a green MVV sticker in the window. On the machines are lists of destinations and the appropriate number of strips you have to cancel. Tickets must be cancelled in machines at the entrance to the stations or on board the buses and trams.

For people using transport very often on any given day, the day-ticket (Tageskarte), valid until 6am the following day, is highly recommended. The Single-Tageskarte for DM8.50 (children under 15, DM3) is valid for the inner city area; the Single-Tageskarte for DM17 (children DM5) is valid for the *entire* public transport area. The Partner-Tageskarte can be used by up to five people including two adults and three children, and one dog. For the inner city area or the outer zones it costs DM12.50; for the entire public transport area DM25.

For visitors to Munich who are not using the system enough to need a day-ticket, the MVV (Munich Public Transport) is divided into five zones. Inside the city one trip with a single-journey ticket costs DM3.50, with a blue multiple-journey ticket DM2.80 (two stripes). A single ticket for a short trip (up to four stops, only two of which may be with the U- or S-Bahn) costs DM1.80, with a blue multiple-journey ticket DM1.40 (one stripe). Inside the city children from four to 15 pay DM1.50 for a single-journey ticket, with a children's multiple-journey ticket DM1.10 (one stripe).

Taxis

Taxi stands can be found all over the city. If you want to call a taxi (Central Office, tel: 2161-0), it is advisable to have a look at the inside front cover of the telephone book; there are different numbers for the different quarters of the city. The basic charge is DM3.60, every kilometre DM2.20. Call-Cars and Mini Cars, which offer better value for the money, cannot be hailed on the street and must be booked by phone, tel: 723 8711, 555333, 555444 and 558383.

Facts for the Visitor

Visas

Visas are not required for citizens of European Community countries; a valid identity card or passport is enough to ensure entry and exit. Holders of Australian, Canadian, Japanese, New Zealand, South African and US passports automatically get three-month permits on crossing the border but visas are required for longer stays.

Customs

Non-EC members can bring 400 cigarettes, one bottle of spirits, two of wine and 50g of perfume; EC-members have guide levels of 800 cigarettes, 10 litres of spirit and 90 litres of wine. Customs keep a close watch for drugs.

Tourist information

For information before you leave home, contact the offices of the German National Tourist Office.

UK: German National Tourist Office, Nightingale House, 65 Curzon Street, London W1Y 7PE, tel: (0891) 600100, fax: (0171) 495 6129.

US: German National Tourist Office, 444 South Flower Street, Suite 2230, Los Angeles CA 90071, tel: (213) 688 7332, fax: (213) 688 7574; Chanin Building, 122 East 42nd Street, 52nd floor, New York, NY 10168, tel: (212) 308 3300, fax: (212) 688 1322.

For information when you are in Munich:

The Tourismus-Information (Tourist Office), in the town hall, provides advice on all questions about staying in Munich (Monday to Friday 10am–8pm, Saturday 10am–4pm, tel: 233 03272/3). Further branches of the Tourist Office are to be found at the Main Station, Bahnhofsplatz 2 (Monday to Saturday 10am–8pm, Sunday 10am–6pm, tel: 233 30256/7) and in the arrivals hall at the airport (Monday to Friday 10am–9pm, Saturday and Sunday noon–8pm, tel: 9759 2815)

For advice on the surrounding region, contact the *Tourismusverband München-Oberbayern* (Munich and Upper Bavaria Tourist Association), Bodenseestrasse 113, tel: 829218-0. Further information on the Alps can be obtained from the *Deutscher Alpenverein* (German Alpine Club), Praterinsel 5, tel: 294940.

The English-language magazine *Munich Found* is a valuable source of information for English-speaking visitors and is available from most newsagents.

Currency and exchange

The basic unit of German currency is the mark (DM), divided into 100 pfennigs. Coins come in 1, 2, 5, 10 marks and 50 pfennig denominations, as well as 1, 2, and 5 marks; notes start at 10 and go upwards.

Foreign currency can be changed into German marks at all banks and savings banks, as well as in large hotels. There is also no shortage of *Wechselstuben* (bureaux de change). Banks and savings banks are usually open from 8.30am to 12.30pm and from 1.30 to 3.30pm (Thursday until 5.30pm). There are banks which are also open at weekends at the main railway station (daily 6am–11pm) and at the airport, daily 7am–8.30pm.

Sightseeing tours

Guided sightseeing tours are run regularly by the **Münchner Stadtrundfahrten OHG**, Arnulfstrasse 8, tel: 120 4248. The tours begin at Bahnhofsplatz in front of the department store Hertie:

Short tour (1 hour), daily 10am, 11.30am and 2.30pm.

City tour (2½ hours), 10am and 2.30pm daily, including a visit to the Olympic Park.

Extended tour (2½ hours), 10am daily except Monday including St Peter's Church and the Alte Pinakothek, or 12.30pm including a visit to Nymphenburg Palace.

Radius Touristik organises city tours by bicycle, walking tours of the old part of the city, and theme tours, daily, tel: 43660383.

City Hopper Tours offers city tours by bicycle, Tuesday to Sunday from 10am, reservations, tel: 2721131.

Stattreisen München eV, tel. 2718940, offers special theme tours, district tours and children's tours.

Bavaria film tours

Bavariafilmplatz 7, Geiselgasteig. On the tour through Germany's film town, the main attractions are the *Berliner*

Strasse, scene of many films; the U-boat, famous for its role in *The Boat*; and the mine, *Rote Erde*, typical of the Ruhr district. Tours from 1 April to 31 October, daily from 9am to 4pm. Admission fee: DM11 for adults, DM7 for children, school groups and handicapped people.

Tipping
Even though service is now officially included everywhere, tipping is still customary and bills are rounded off.

Opening times
In Munich, as in the rest of Germany, business hours are strictly controlled. Shops are generally open from 8 or 9am to 6pm, except on Thursday when they can remain open until 8 or 8.30pm. On Saturdays, they close at 1 or 2pm, except for the first Saturday of the month, *langer Samstag*, when stores in the city centre are open until 4pm. All that is open on Sunday are some bakeries which double as cafés, and shops at the railway station or airport which charge exorbitant prices.

Public holidays
1 January (New Year); 6 January (Epiphany); Shrove Tuesday; Good Friday; Easter Monday; 1 May (May Day); Ascension Day; Whit Monday; Corpus Christi; 15 August (The Assumption); 3 October (German Unification Day); 1 November (All Souls' Day); Day of Prayer and Repentence; 25 December (Christmas Day); 26 December (Boxing Day).

Postal services
Post offices are generally open Monday to Friday 8am–6pm, Saturday 8am–noon. Postfiliale 31, Bahnhofsplatz (in the main station) has longer opening times (Monday to Friday 7am–8pm, Saturday 8am–4pm, Sundays and holidays 9am–3pm, tel: 552262-0/10). At Postfiliale 1, Residenzstrasse 2, tel: 290387-10/1 there is an express mail service, a public fax office and exchange available. At the airport a post office is located in the central hall of the main terminal building (Monday to Saturday 8am–9pm, Sunday 10am–1pm and 2–7.30pm).

Stamps can be obtained from post offices or the automatic machines outside. The post boxes, like the telephone boxes, are bright yellow.

Telephoning
Pay telephones are easily accessible, solidly built, and accept 10-pfennig, 1-mark and 5-mark coins. As in most European cities, long-distance telephone calls can be made from the post office, which saves you having to pay the hefty surcharges levied by hotels. To call other countries,

first dial the international access code 00, then the relevant country code as follows: Australia 61; France 33; Japan 81; Netherlands 31; Spain 34; United Kingdom 44; US and Canada 1. If using a US phone credit card, dial the company's access number: AT &T, tel: 0130-0010; MCI, tel: 0130-0012; Sprint, tel: 0130-0013. The code for Germany is 49, for Munich 089.

Time
Germany is six hours ahead of US Eastern Standard Time and one ahead of Greenwich Mean Time.

Medical
Visitors from the EU have the right to claim health services available to Germans. UK visitors should obtain Form E111 from the Department of Health.

Chemists are open daily Monday to Saturday noon. The addresses of chemists open at weekends are posted on the doors. In case of need: Bahnhof Apotheke (international), Bahnhofplatz 2, tel: 594119. Europaapotheke, Schützenstrasse 12, tel: 595423. Internationale Ludwigs Apotheke, Neuhauser Strasse 8, tel: 260 8011.

In case of more serious ailments, contact the Universitätspoliklinik (University Clinic), Pettenkoferstrasse 8a, tel: 5160-0.

Emergency numbers
Police, tel: 110.
Fire-brigade, tel: 112.
Ambulance, tel: 112.
Emergency chemist, tel: 594475.
Emergency medical attention, tel: 551771.

Lost and found
City: Ötztaler Strasse 17, tel:233 45900. Monday to Friday 8.30am–noon, Tuesday also 2–5.30pm.

Railway: Hauptbahnhof, Bahnhofplatz 2 (opposite platform 26), tel: 128 5859.

S-Bahn: Ostbahnhof, tel: 12884/409. Monday to Friday 8am–5.45pm, Saturday 8am–11.45pm.

Diplomatic missions
American Consulate, Königinstrasse 5, tel: 23011.

British Consulate-General, Amalienstrasse 62, tel: 394015.

Libraries are available at the British Council, Rosenheimer Strasse 116b, tel: 401832 and the Amerika-Haus, Karolinenplatz 3, tel: 595369.

In addition, a large choice of English-language books can be found in the main municipal library at the Gasteig Culture Centre.

Accommodation

Booking in advance is recommended, particularly in the summer months, during the Oktoberfest, or in *Fasching* (the carnival season). A single room costs between DM60 and DM480, according to hotel category; a double room between DM90 and DM680. Accommodation Service and Information is available in the main railway station, daily 8am–10pm, Sunday 11am–7pm (no telephone accommodation service); Rindermarkt/Pettenbeckstrasse, tel: 2391-272, Monday to Friday 9.30am–6pm; at the airport (main building), tel: 9759 2815, Monday to Saturday 8.30am–10pm, Sunday and public holidays 1–9pm.

$$$$$

Bayerischer Hof, Promenadeplatz 2–6, tel: 21200; **Hilton City**, Rosenheimer Strasse 15, tel: 48040; **Hilton Park**, Am Tucherpark 7, tel: 38450; **Kempinski Hotel Vier Jahreszeiten**, Maximilianstrasse 17, tel: 21250; **Der Königshof**, Karlsplatz 25, tel: 551360; **Marriott München**, Berliner Strasse 93, tel: 360020; **Mercure**, Senefelderstrasse 9, tel: 551320; **Rafael**, Neuturmstrasse 1, tel: 290980; **Sheraton**, Arabellastrasse 6, tel: 92640.

$$$$

Arabella Bogenhausen, Arabellastrasse 5, tel: 92320; **Arabella Olympiapark**, Helene-Mayer-Ring 12, tel: 3516071; **Arabella Westpark**, Garmischer Strasse 2, tel: 51960; **Eden-Hotel-Wolff**, Arnulfstrasse 4–8, tel: 551150; **Erzgiesserei Europe**, Erzgiessereistrasse 15, tel: 126820; **Excelsior**, Schützenstrasse 11, tel: 551370; **Forum**, Hoch-

strasse 3, tel: 48030; **Holiday Inn Crowne Plaza**, Leopoldstrasse 200, tel: 381790; **International**, Hohen-zollernstrasse 9, tel: 398001; **Intercity-Hotel**, at the main station, tel: 545560. **Maritim**, Goethestrasse 7, tel: 552350; **Palace**, Trogerstrasse 21, tel: 419710; **München City Hilton**, Rosenheimer Str. 15, tel: 4804-0; **München Park Hilton**, Am Tucherpark 7, tel: 3845-0; **Preysing**, Preysingstrasse 1, tel: 458450; **Regent**, Seidlstrasse 2, tel: 551590; **Renaissance-München Hotel**, Theodor-Dombart Strasse 4, tel: 360990.

$$$

Admiral, Kohlstrasse 9, tel: 226641; **Ambassador Parkhotel**, Plinganserstrasse 102, tel: 724890; **An der Oper**, Falkenturmstrasse 10, tel: 2900270; **Astoria**, Nikolaistr.9, tel: 3839630; **Atrium**, Landwehrstr 59, tel: 51419-0; **Carlton**, Fürstenstrasse 12, tel: 282061; **Bristol**, Pettenkoferstrasse 2, tel: 595151; **City**, Schillerstrasse 3a, tel: 558091; **Concorde**, Herrnstrasse 38, tel: 224515; **Domus**, St-Anna-Strasse 31, tel: 221704; **Drei Löwen**, Schillerstrasse 8, tel: 551040; **Europäischer Hof**, Bayerstrasse 31, tel: 551510; **Haberstock**, Schillerstrasse 4, tel: 557855. **Ibis**, Ungererstrasse 139, tel: 360830; **Königswache**, Steinheilstrasse 7, tel: 5427750; **Krone**, Theresienhöhe 8, tel: 504052; **Leopold**, Leonpoldstrasse 119, tel: 367061; **Mark**, Senefelderstrasse 12, tel: 559820; **Splendid**, Maximilianstrasse 54, tel: 296606.

$$

Adler, Ledererstrasse 8, tel: 223 9912; **Alfa**, Hirtenstrasse 22, tel: 5459530; **Amba**, Arnulfstrasse 20, tel: 545140; **Blauer Bock**, Blumenstrasse 16, tel: 231780; **Dachs**, Amalienstrasse 12, tel: 282086; **Daniel**, Sonnenstrasse 5, tel: 554945; **Kraft**, Schillerstrasse 49, tel: 594823; **Kriemhild**, Guntherstrasse 16, tel: 1711170; **Mirabell**, Goethestr. 19a, tel: 551320; **Neuner**, Bergonstr.13a, tel: 8112053.

Youth accommodation

Jugendherberge München (Munich Youth Hostel), Wendl-Dietrich-Strasse 30, tel: 131156; **DJH-Gästehaus Thalkirchen**, Miesingstrasse 4, tel: 72365/60; **Jugendhotel Haus International**, Elisabethstrasse 87, tel: 120-060; **Burg Schwaneck**, Burgweg 4–6, Pullach, tel: 7930643 (easily reachable by S-Bahn).

Camping

Thalkirchen, Zentralländstrasse 49, tel: 7231707; mid-March until the end of October.

Obermenzing, Lochhausener Strasse 59, tel: 8112235; 15 March to 31 October.

Index